CHINA BANKING REGULATORY COMMISSION
2014 ANNUAL REPORT

中国金融出版社
CHINA FINANCIAL PUBLISHING HOUSE

责任编辑：陈　翎
责任校对：李俊英
责任印制：程　颖

图书在版编目（CIP）数据

中国银行业监督管理委员会2014年报（China Banking Regulatory Commission 2014 Annual Report）/中国银行业监督管理委员会宣传部编著. —北京：中国金融出版社，2015.7

ISBN 978 - 7 - 5049 - 8033 - 5

Ⅰ.①中…　Ⅱ.①中…　Ⅲ.①银行监管—中国—2014—年报—英文
Ⅳ.①F832.1-54

中国版本图书馆CIP数据核字（2015）第151225号

声明：除特别注明外，本年报数据均为法人口径数据，货币单位均为人民币。
本年报以中文版为准，英文版仅供参考。
本年报由银监会宣传部负责解释。

出版
发行　中国金融出版社

社址　北京市丰台区益泽路2号
市场开发部　（010）63266347，63805472，63439533（传真）
网上书店　http://www.chinafph.com
　　　　　　（010）63286832，63365686（传真）
读者服务部　（010）66070833，62568380
邮编　100071
经销　新华书店
印刷　天津银博印刷集团有限公司
尺寸　209毫米×297毫米
印张　11.5
字数　304千
版次　2015年7月第1版
印次　2015年7月第1次印刷
定价　118.00元
ISBN 978 - 7 - 5049 - 8033 - 5/F. 7593
如出现印装错误本社负责调换　联系电话（010）63263947

CONTENTS

Chairman's Statement   **6**

About the CBRC   **9**

I. Our mandates, objectives & missions   9

II. Our philosophy, approach & criteria   9

III. Code of Conduct   9

IV. Management   10

V. Special Advisor   12

VI. Chief Advisor   12

VII. International Advisory Council (IAC)   12

VIII. Organizational structure   14

Part One   Economic & Banking Developments   **19**

I. Macroeconomic and financial environment   20

II. Latest development of China's banking sector   23

Part Two   Banking Reform and Development   **29**

I. Reform and transformation of the banking sector   30

II.Financial Innovation   44

III.Opening-up   47

**Part Three   Supporting Economic Restructuring,
              Transformation and Upgrading**   **53**

I. Tapping the idle capital while making good use of incremental capital   54

II. Financial support to key areas and industries   57

III. Financial inclusion   63

IV. Addressing overcapacity and promoting green credit   72

V. Fully promoting balanced regional development   75

Part Four   Enhancing Law-based Regulation to Strengthen Supervisory Capability   **81**

I. Building Supervisory Framework   82

II. Supervisory approaches   84

III. Supervisory cooperation and coordination   91

IV. Organizational development   93

Part Five   Prudential Regulation   **101**

I. Macro-prudential regulation   102

II. Corporate governance and internal controls   104

III. Capital regulation   105

IV. Credit risk supervision   107

V. Liquidity risk supervision   111

VI. Operational risk supervision   113

VII. IT risk supervision   115

VIII. Market risk supervision   116

IX. Country risk supervision   116

X. Reputational risk supervision   117

Part Six   Banking Consumer Protection and Education   **119**

I. Development of regulatory framework   120

II. Promoting banking institutions to fulfill their duties   122

III. Promoting financial literacy   123

IV. Strengthening consumer protection survey and research   125

Part Seven   Strengthening Transparency and Market Discipline   **127**

I. Enhancing information disclosure   128

II. Improving transparency of the banking sector   129

III. Strengthening market discipline   129

Part Eight   Social Responsibility   **133**

I. Guiding banking institutions to strengthen CSR   134

II. Promoting the sustainable development of student loans   134

III. Securing quality financial services during public holidays   135

IV. Supporting disaster relief and post-disaster reconstruction   136

V. Supporting charity and poverty-stricken areas   137

Part Nine   Outlook   **141**

I. Economic and financial outlook   142

II. Supervisory focuses in 2015   142

Part Ten Appendixes 147

Appendix 1   Responsibility description of the CBRC departments and local offices   148

Appendix 2   Financial management activities of the CBRC   153

Appendix 3   Rules and regulatory documents issued in 2014   154

Appendix 4   MOUs and EOLs with overseas regulators   156

Appendix 5   Significant regulatory and supervisory events in 2014   159

Appendix 6   Terminology   166

Part Eleven Statistics 169

Appendix 1   Total assets of banking institutions (2003-2014)   170

Appendix 2   Total liabilities of banking institutions (2003-2014)   171

Appendix 3   Total owner's equity of banking institutions (2003-2014)   172

Appendix 4   Total deposits and loans of banking institutions (2003-2014)   173

Appendix 5   Profit after tax of banking institutions (2007-2014)   173

Appendix 6   Returns of banking institutions (2007-2014)   174

Appendix 7   NPLs of banking institutions (2010-2014)   174

Appendix 8   Liquidity ratio of banking institutions (2007-2014)   174

Appendix 9   NPLs, asset impairment provisions and provisioning
              coverage ratio of commercial banks (2007-2014)   175

Appendix 10   NPLs of commercial banks (2014)   175

Appendix 11   Distribution of NPLs of commercial banks by industry (2014)   176

Appendix 12   Distribution of NPLs of commercial banks by region (2014)   177

Appendix 13   CAR of commercial banks (2010-2014)   178

Appendix 14   CAR of commercial banks (2013-2014)   178

Appendix 15   CBRC on-site examinations (2003-2014)   179

Appendix 16   Number of legal entities and staff of banking institutions
              (As of end-2014)   180

Thematic columns

Thematic column 1   Private capital participating in the banking sector   34

Thematic column 2   Improving credit availability and affordability for enterprises   55

Thematic column 3   The development of banking industry in China
                    (Shanghai) Pilot Free Trade Zone (SFTZ)   58

Thematic column 4   The 18th ICBS held in Tianjin   92

Boxes

Box 1   Progress in the international financial regulatory reform   21

Box 2   Improving interbank business and wealth management business governance   30

Box 3   Creation of the Trust Protection Fund   40

Box 4   Consumer finance companies boosted the consumption of low and

	medium-income groups	43
Box 5	Commercial banks commenced the pilot program of "direct financing tools for wealth management"	44
Box 6	Banks taking initiative to meet interest rate liberalization	46
Box 7	Opening-up of the mainland China's banking sector to foreign-owned banks	49
Box 8	Further opening-up of the mainland China's banking sector to Hong Kong and Macau	49
Box 9	Further deepening the cross-strait banking cooperation	50
Box 10	The pilot project of credit asset securitization made positive progress	54
Box 11	Supporting the creation of the National Integrated Circuit(IC) Industry Fund	62
Box 12	Banking institutions supported the development of E-commerce in rural areas	64
Box 13	Promoting rural financial development and unleashing vitality	68
Box 14	The CBRC issued the *Key Performance Indicators for Implementing Green Gredit*	74
Box 15	Promoting law-based regulation in the banking sector	83
Box 16	The CBRC issued the *Guidelines on Supervisory Ratings of Commercial Banks*	87
Box 17	The CBRC deployed and carried out "two strengthening and two curbing" campaign	89
Box 18	Examining the application of EAST	89
Box 19	Key on-site examination projects	89
Box 20	Socialist core value education campaign	95
Box 21	Organizational work of provincial Youth League Work Committees made all-round breakthroughs	96
Box 22	Issuing *Guidelines on Disclosing Assessment Indicators of Global Systemic Importance of Commercial Banks*	103
Box 23	Issuing the *Guidelines on Internal Controls of Commercial Banks*	104
Box 24	Non-performing loans (NPLs) of commercial banks	109
Box 25	Issuing the *Notice on Adjusting Loan-to-Deposit Calculation Methods of Commercial Banks*	111
Box 26	Issuing the *Rules on Liquidity Risk Management of Commercial Banks*	112
Box 27	Preventing and mitigating IT outsourcing risks of the banking sector	116
Box 28	The High-level banking consumer protection steering committee was established	121
Box 29	The CBRC strengthened the financial literacy publicity in rural areas	124
Box 30	Large commercial banks ensuring the continued delivery of financial services during the Chinese New Year holiday	135
Box 31	The CBRC launched "5 Ones" initiative for young financial employees to help people with disabilities	138

Media perspective

Media perspective 1   To open the "right door" for interbank business, new
                      regulations push ahead the financial service industry   31

Media perspective 2   The first 5 private bank Pilots Program was selected,
                      involving 10 private investors   36

Media perspective 3   The promulgation of the *Rules for the Administration of the*
                      Trust Protection Fund creates a "safety net" for the trust sector   41

Media perspective 4   The CBRC established the Financial Inclusion Affairs
                      Department to guide the sound development of P2P lending   72

Media perspective 5   More flexible LTD ratio for credit loosening   112

Charts

Chart 1   Total assets and liabilities of banking institutions (2003-2014)   24

Chart 2   Market share (by assets) of banking institutions (2003-2014)   24

Chart 3   Deposits, loans & loan-to-deposit ratio (2003-2014)   25

Chart 4   NPL ratio of commercial banks (2007-2014)   26

Chart 5   Asset impairment provisions and provisioning coverage ratio (2007-2014)   26

Chart 6   Income structure of banking institutions (2014)   27

Chart 7   Liquidity condition of banking institutions (January to December 2014)   27

Chart 8   Breakdown of loans to strategic emerging industries by 21 major banks as
           of end-2014   60

Chart 9   Breakdown of loans to key areas in the culture industry by 21 major
           banks as of end-2014   60

Table 1   Foreign banking establishments in China (As of end-2014)   48

Table 2   Foreign banking assets in China (2010-2014)   48

Chairman's Statement

2014 was an extraordinary year for the banking industry. China dealt with the slowdown in economic growth, made difficult structural adjustments and absorbed the effects of previous economic stimulus policies simultaneously. Under the leadership of the CPC Central Committee and the State Council, China's banking sector gained notable progress in banking reform, supervision and development.

The awareness of reform was strengthened to inject new vitality into growth and development. President Xi Jinping stressed that we should be quick yet steady in comprehensively deepening the reform and stay committed to what we set our sights on. Thus, we think twice before embarking on our endeavor to further advance reform and opening up of the banking industry. Private capital was further encouraged to tap the banking sector, with historic breakthrough made in the private bank pilot program and the establishment of a batch of private-capital-dominated financial leasing companies, consumer finance companies, finance companies and village and township banks. The reform initiatives on reinforcing the corporate, business, risk and industry governance systems were advanced, commercial banks urged to set up inter-bank business units and wealth management business units, and Trust Protection Fund and the governing body set up. On the front of opening-up, rules governing foreign banks were amended, while reform and innovation of the banking operations in China (Shanghai) Pilot Free Trade Zone were conducted to enhance the extent of openness to Hong Kong- and Macau-based banks marked by pre-licensing national treatment plus negative list. Moreover, the CBRC successfully held the 18th International Conference of Banking Supervisors, fully exhibiting to the international community what had been achieved in the banking reform and supervisory development.

The awareness of keeping the bigger picture in mind was enhanced to actively boost the implementation of key national strategies. Since the 18th Party Congress, the new central leadership demonstrated ambitious vision and exceptional courage and masterminded a series of new national strategies. We actively guided banking institutions to act in response to trends, develop strategic visions, keep the bigger picture in mind, and grasp the strategic opportunities opened by the deepening of international economic cooperation, transformation and upgrading of the national economy. The banking industry was encouraged to make use of their financial resources to support the implementation of three major strategies, i.e. the Belt and Road Initiative, coordinated development of Beijing, Tianjin and Hebei, and Yangtze River Economic Belt Initiative, to help Chinese industries, companies and equipment sector to "go global", and support the implementation of the Innovation-driven Development Strategy and major industrial development strategies. As the country was implementing important strategies, we also guided banks to seek respective niche markets so as to explore untapped market potentials and pursue new growth points.

The service awareness was reinforced to highlight the significance of financial sector serving the real economy. Since last year, the downward pressure on economy had been trending up. Premier Li Keqiang reckoned that the financial sector should play an active role in meeting the needs of the real economy, including that of small and micro businesses, agriculture, rural areas, and farmers. In response, we guided banking institutions to tap their idle funds, make good use of incremental funds and improve the quality of credit, thereby boosting the steady and sound development of the real economy. We further strengthened the incentive and restraint mechanism, guiding banking institutions to implement differentiated credit policies and strengthen credit support for key industries and projects. The methodology of computing loan-to-deposit ratio was revised and special financial bonds were allowed for issuance, thereby facilitating the tilt of banking support towards three rural undertakings (i.e. agriculture, rural areas and farmers), MSEs and other weak areas. The full coverage of basic financial services was consolidated, together with financial service charges and fees well regulated, rights and interests of financial consumers protected and financial inclusion developed, thereby constantly improving the satisfaction and availability of financial services.

The awareness of risk prevention and control was enhanced to firmly hold the bottom line of keeping systemic regional financial risks at bay. In the face of increasing risks and pressure, we stayed calm and took a number of actions to hold the bottom line. We watched closely risk events that had occurred, and took timely and effective measures strictly against contingency plans. We stringently controlled potential risks, implemented risk control accountability, and fended off the transmission and contagion of risks resulted from excess capacity, local government funding platforms, real estate loans, inter-bank transactions, wealth management business and shadow banking. The lines of defense regarding capital, provisioning and management were further reinforced, channels for capital replenishment expanded, and inspection over the quality and authenticity of assets strengthened, thus enhancing the banking industry's intrinsic risk resistance capability. Over the past year, the banking industry has seen steady progress in terms of key supervisory indicators. The NPL ratio of banking institutions remained at a low level of 1.6 percent, while the provisioning coverage ratio maintained as high as 191.8 percent. The capital adequacy ratio increased to 13.2 percent, up 0.99 percentage point year on year.

The awareness for rule of law was stepped up to raise the level of compliant operations and supervision by law. Since the rule of law serves as the foundation for the banking sector development, we called for compliant banking operations in accordance with applicable rules and regulation and the observance of "Three Iron Spirits" (i.e. iron account book, iron abacus and iron rules and regulations) so that banking institutions could become compliant market players. No less emphasis was made on the front of conducting supervision by law, streamlining administration and delegating powers with a number of licensing matters exempted and substantial licensing power delegated to local offices. The supervisory rules framework was further improved through the newly issued rules and regulations, including the **Rules on Liquidity Risk Management of Commercial Banks (Provisional)**, and post-assessment and check-up of all supervisory rules and regulations adopted after the establishment of the CBRC. Improvements were also made to supervisory approaches, classified supervision, consolidated supervision and the enriching of supervisory indicator system. We improved the supervisory enforcement capability, strictly executed supervisory penalties, firmly fought against illegal fundraising and cracked down on illegal financial organizations to constantly enhance the supervisory effectiveness.

The awareness of enforcing strict Party discipline was strengthened, with work styles improved and discipline strictly observed. As the Party was implementing the mass line education practice, we took the opportunity to improve the work styles of the banking industry. We strictly followed the eight-point regulation, cleaned up four undesirable work styles (i.e. formalism, bureaucracy, hedonism and extravagance), and promoted the long-term work styles improvement mechanism. We implemented the system of accountability for improving Party conduct and upholding integrity under which the Party committees shouldered the major responsibility, and the Party commission for discipline inspection was in charge of supervision. The Party's disciplinary requirements were also strictly implemented and a well-disciplined supervisory team was developed with a fine work style.

Currently, China's economy gradually adjusts to the new normal with slower growth, continued restructuring and changed economic gear. As President Xi Jinping pointed out, the new normal would present both new opportunities and new conflicts, coupled with potential risks. Whether the banking industry can have steady performance and growth under the new normal depends on how determined and committed we are to adapting ourselves to the new normal, making new reforms and seeking new development.

In 2015, the CBRC will take the lead to reform the supervisory regime through undertaking supervisory restructuring, highlighting main supervisory functions, streamlining administration and delegating powers so as to give effective supervisory underpinning to the reform and development of the banking industry under the new normal. As an old saying goes, "if you renew yourself for one day, you can renew yourself daily, and continue to do so." In face of the new situation, we will continue to make explorations and blaze new trails of our supervisory work on such fronts as comprehensively strengthening party construction, comprehensively facilitating banking reform and opening up, comprehensively promoting the rule of law, comprehensively strengthening financial risk supervision, comprehensively improving banking industry's capability in serving the real economy, thereby pushing the banking industry to make leap-frog developments and making contribution to the realization of the "two centenary goals" and the Chinese Dream.

尚福林

Chairman SHANG Fulin
China Banking Regulatory Commission
May 2015

About the CBRC

I. Our mandates, objectives & missions

Mandates: Regulating and supervising banking institutions and their business operations in China.

Objectives: To protect fair competition in the banking sector and enhance the industry's competitiveness, and thereby promoting the safety and soundness of the banking sector and maintaining public confidence in the banking sector.

Supervisory missions: Protecting the interests of depositors and other customers and maintaining public confidence in the banking sector through prudential supervision; increasing public knowledge about modern financial products, services and the related risks through education and information disclosure; and reducing banking-related crimes to maintain financial stability.

II. Our philosophy, approach & criteria

Principle: Supervision by law, and supervision for the people.

Supervisory philosophy: Conducting consolidated supervision, ensuring the supervised institutions having in place effective risk management and internal control systems, and enhancing transparency.

Supervisory approach: Conducting risk-based prudential supervision to ensure accurate loan classification, sufficient loss provisioning, appropriate write-offs, acceptable profitability and adequate capital of banking institutions.

Supervisory criteria: Enabling financial stability while facilitating financial innovation; enhancing the international competitiveness of the banking sector; setting scientific and appropriate supervisory criteria and standards and refraining from unnecessary restrictions; encouraging fair and orderly competition; subjecting both the supervisors and supervised institutions to a strict and well-defined system of accountability; and allocating supervisory resources in a cost-efficient manner.

III. Code of Conduct

In performing their official duties, the CBRC staff must:

1. NOT interfere in regulated banking institutions' credit (including loans, guarantees, acceptances and discounts), asset disposal and project investment activities;

2. NOT interfere in the internal affairs of regulated banking institutions, such as human resources, constructions and bidding process; and

3. NOT accept any advantages from regulated banking institutions, such as servings, entertainments, vacations, cash, valuable securities, certificates of payments and other valuable gifts.

IV. Management

Chairman SHANG Fulin
Responsible for the overall work of the CBRC.

Vice Chairman
ZHOU Mubing

Responsible for the supervision of large commercial banks, rural commercial banks, rural cooperative banks, rural credit cooperatives and new-type rural financial institutions, overseeing activities related to policy research, financial inclusion, anti-illegal fund raising (banking security & safeguard), and the coordination with the China Financing Guarantee Association and the China Micro-credit Companies Association.

Vice Chairman
GUO Ligen

Responsible for the supervision of banking information technology, overseeing the CBRC's on-site examination, human resources management, the activities of the CPC Committee of the CBRC Headquarters, the Party School, the CBRC Staff Union, the CBRC Youth League Committee and the China Financial Staff Union.

Vice Chairman
WANG Zhaoxing

Responsible for the supervision of policy banks and foreign-funded banking institutions, overseeing activities related to prudential regulation, banking consumer protection, international affairs, and the coordination with the Large Financial Institutions Supervisory Board.

Disciplinary Commissioner
DU Jinfu

Responsible for the CBRC staff compliance and inspection.

Vice Chairman
CAO Yu

Responsible for legal & regulation affairs, the supervision of business and product innovation activities, joint-stock commercial banks, and city commercial banks, overseeing the CBRC accounting activities, the staff service function, affairs of the education center in Langfang, and the coordination with the China Central Depository & Clearing Co., Ltd..

Assistant Chairman
YANG Jiacai

Responsible for the supervision of trust companies and other non-bank financial institutions, overseeing the CBRC's administrative affairs, publicity, and the coordination with the China Banking Association, the China Trustee Association, the China National Finance Companies Association, and the China Rural Finance Magazine.

Acknowledgement to YAN Qingmin, former Vice Chairman of the CBRC (left in December 2014)

V. Special Advisor

YANG Kaisheng

Former President of the Industrial and Commercial Bank of China (ICBC).

VI. Chief Advisor

Mr. Andrew Sheng

Former Chairman of the Hong Kong Securities and Futures Commission.

VII. International Advisory Council (IAC)

Established with the approval from the State Council, the IAC of the CBRC consists of well-known international financial specialists. The IAC provides consulting services on issues related to long-term development strategies of Chinese banking sector and banking supervision. The IAC members meet on a regular base.

Foreign IAC members

Mr. Andrew Sheng

Chief Advisor of the CBRC, former Chairman of the Hong Kong Securities and Futures Commission.

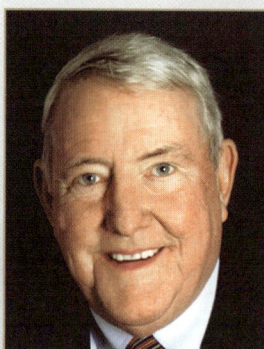

Mr. Gerald Corrigan

Chairman of Goldman Sachs Bank USA, former President of the New York Federal Reserve Bank.

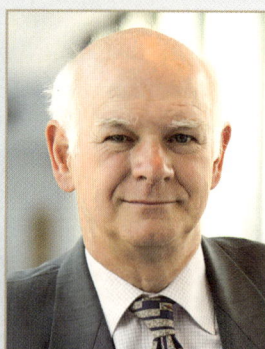

Sir Howard Davies

Director of Prudential PLC, Director of Morgan Stanley, former Director of London School of Economics and Political Science, former Chairman of the U.K. Financial Services Authority.

Mr. Roger Ferguson

President and CEO of TIAA-CREF, former Vice Chairman of the Board of Governors of the Federal Reserve System (FED), former voting member of the Federal Open Market Committee, and former Chairman of the Financial Stability Forum.

Mr. Ian Macfarlane

Non-executive Director of the ANZ Bank, former Governor of the Reserve Bank of Australia.

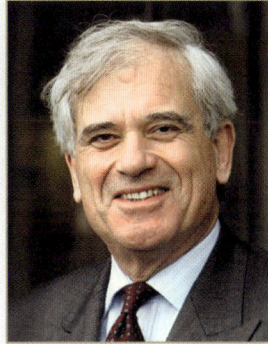

Mr. Tom de Swaan

Chairman of the Audit Committee of Glaxo Smith Kline, former Chairman of the Basel Committee on Banking Supervision (BCBS).

Ms. Sheila Bair

Chairman of the Systemic Risk Council, Senior Advisor to the Pew Charitable Trusts, former Chairman of Federal Deposit Insurance Corporation (FDIC).

Mr. Stuart Gulliver

Group Chief Executive of HSBC Holdings plc.

Mr. Jean-Claude Trichet

Former Governor of the bank of France, former President of the European Central Bank.

Ms. Laura Cha

Chairman of Hongkong's Financial Services Development Council, Member of Executive Council of Hong Kong, Non-Executive Director of the Hongkong and Shanghai Banking Corporation(HSBC), former Deputy Chairman of Hongkong's Securities and Futures Commission, and former Vice Chairman of the China Securities Regulatory Commission (CSRC).

Former IAC members

Mr. Josef Ackermann	President of Zurich Insurance Group, former CEO of Deutsche Bank.
Sir John Bond	Chairman of Xstrata PLC, former Chairman of the HSBC Holdings plc., former Chairman of Vodafone Group.

VIII. Organizational structure

As of end-2014, the CBRC departments and local offices include: various departments at the CBRC headquarters (listed below), Supervisory Boards, the China Financial Staff Union, 36 provincial offices, 306 field offices and 1,730 supervisory agencies. In addition, the CBRC maintains 4 training centers in Beidaihe, Shenyang, Shunde and Langfang.

1.Head Office

Department	Person in Charge
General Office	YANG Jiacai
Policy Research Bureau	LIU Chunhang
Prudential Regulation Bureau	XIAO Yuanqi
On-site Examination Bureau	HAN Yi
Legal Department	LIU Fushou
Financial Inclusion Department	LI Junfeng
Banking Information Technology Supervision Department	XIE Chongda
Banking Innovation Supervision Department	WANG Yanxiu
Banking Consumer Protection Department	DENG Zhiyi
Policy Bank Supervision Department	ZHOU Minyuan
Large Commercial Bank Supervision Department	YANG Liping (Ms)
National Joint-stock Commercial Bank Supervision Department	YU Longwu
City Commercial Bank Supervision Department	LING Gan
Rural Financial Institution Supervision Department	JIANG Liming (Ms)
Foreign Bank Supervision Department	DUAN Jining (Ms)

Department	Person in Charge
Trust Institution Supervision Department	LI Fuan
Non-bank Financial Institution Supervision Department	LI Fuan
Anti-illegal Fund Raising Office (Banking Security & Safeguard Bureau)	YANG Yuzhu
Accounting Department	HU Yongkang
International Department (Office of Hong Kong, Macau & Taiwan Affairs)	FAN Wenzhong
Staff Compliance & Disciplinary Bureau	CHEN Qiong (Ms)
Human Resources Department	XIAO Pu
Publicity & Information Department	MEI Zhixiang (Acting Head)
CBRC Headquarters CPC Committee	JIE Hongwei
Party School	PAN Guangwei
CBRC Staff Union	ZHANG Dongfeng
Financial Youth League Committee	GUO Hong
Headquarters Service Center	ZHANG Zhongqi

Note: As of the date of 2014 Annual Report publishment.

2. Provincial Offices

CBRC Offices	Person in Charge
The CBRC Beijing Office	SU Baoxiang
The CBRC Tianjin Office	YU Longwu
The CBRC Hebei Office	LI Lichun
The CBRC Shanxi Office	LIU Xiaoyong
The CBRC Inner Mongolia Office	WEN Zhenxin
The CBRC Liaoning Office	LI Lin
The CBRC Jilin Office	GAO Fei
The CBRC Heilongjiang Office	ZHAO Jiangping
The CBRC Shanghai Office	LIAO Min
The CBRC Jiangsu Office	FU Minggao
The CBRC Zhejiang Office	XIONG Tao
The CBRC Anhui Office	TIAN Jianhua
The CBRC Fujian Office	ZHAO Jie
The CBRC Jiangxi Office	LI Hu
The CBRC Shandong Office	CHEN Yulin
The CBRC Henan Office	WANG Zeping
The CBRC Hubei Office	LAI Xiufu
The CBRC Hunan Office	LI Saihui

CBRC Offices	Person in Charge
The CBRC Guangdong Office	WANG Zhanfeng
The CBRC Guangxi Office	ZENG Xiangyang (Ms)
The CBRC Hainan Office	CHEN Gangming
The CBRC Chongqing Office	MA Zhongfu
The CBRC Sichuan Office	WANG Junquan
The CBRC Guizhou Office	GUO Wuping
The CBRC Yunnan Office	CHENG Keng
The CBRC Tibet Office	LI Mingxiao
The CBRC Shaanxi Office	LING Gan
The CBRC Gansu Office	LENG Yunzhu (Ms)
The CBRC Qinghai Office	QIN Hanfeng
The CBRC Ningxia Office	AN Ning
The CBRC Xinjiang Office	WANG Junshou
The CBRC Dalian Office	YUAN Fei
The CBRC Ningbo Office	JI Ming
The CBRC Xiamen Office	ZHANG Anshun
The CBRC Qingdao Office	CHEN Ying (Ms)
The CBRC Shenzhen Office	WANG Xiaohui

Note: As of the date of 2014 Annual Report publishment.

Photograph by the CBRC staff

Part One

Economic & Banking Developments

- Macroeconomic and financial environment
- Latest development of China's banking sector

I. Macroeconomic and financial environment

1. International economic and financial environment

In 2014, the world economy grew by 3.3 percent, remaining at the same level with that of 2013. The commodity price of international trade went up, while growth of trading volume in real terms declined. The trade in goods and service increased by 3.1 percent, representing a year-on-year decrease of 0.3 percentage point [1]. The world economic recovery was uneven, with world economies growing at varied rates. The landscape of global monetary policies became more complicated, with notable divergence in economies. Geopolitical conflicts remain unresolved, exerting significant impact on the economic growth.

Firstly, developed countries experienced a moderate recovery with obvious divergence. In 2014, developed economies grew by 1.8 percent, up 0.5 percentage point year-on-year, but major developed countries saw quite different growth rates, with the United States, euro zone, and Japan growing by 2.4 percent, 0.8 percent and 0.1 percent respectively [2]. In the United States, the economic recovery was stronger than expected. In 2014, the CPI increased by 1.6 percent, slightly higher than 2013 (1.5 percent); the unemployment rate in December was 5.6 percent. The average monthly non-farm payrolls newly added were 260,000, higher than 2013 (195,000) [3]. Turning to the euro zone, affected by slow progress in economic restructuring, pressure on public debt, geopolitical conflicts and other factors, the growth momentum weakened notably. Since July, the year-on-year growth of CPI continued to be lower than 0.5 percent. In December, the CPI saw a negative increase of 0.2 percent year-on-year with technical deflation; by the end of 2014, the unemployment rate was 11.4 percent, with substantial improvement [4]. As for Japan, in terms of three main measures of Abenomics, the effects of stimulative monetary policy and fiscal policy continuously diminished. The negative impact caused by increasing consumption tax exceeded expectations. Compared with last quarter, the GDP growth in the fourth quarter of 2014 rose by 0.49 percent in real terms or 1.5 percent when annualized. The GDP returned to positive growth after two quarters. However, the data was lower than market expectation, indicating that Japanese economy has still not achieved full recovery [5]. Japan might once again face the economic recession; the annual growth of CPI was 2.7 percent, and the economic outlook was uncertain [6].

Secondly, the growth momentum of emerging economies slowed with more complicated risks. Emerging market weakened as a whole. Affected by the strong US dollar and the downturn in commodity prices and other factors, the currencies of emerging economies in 2014 experienced a substantial devaluation. The value of Indonesian Rupiah, Chilean Peso, Brazil Real and Turkey's Lira were close to lowest points over the recent years; the cross-border capital flows were more turbulent. Some emerging economies faced the risk of capital outflows. The statistics from capital flow monitoring institution EPFR (Emerging Portfolio Fund Research) showed that in 2014 the overall

---

[1] International Monetary Fund, **World Economic Outlook**, January 2015.

[2] International Monetary Fund, **World Economic Outlook**, January 2015.

[3] US Department of Labor.

[4] Eurostat.

[5] Japan Cabinet Office, March 9, 2015.

[6] Japan Statistics Bureau, January 30, 2015.

capital outflows of global emerging markets fund were USD23 billion, which was the largest scale of capital outflows since 2011[1]. In addition, growth in emerging market economies also showed differentiated trends. In 2014, the growth of emerging market economies was 4.4 percent, down 0.3 percentage point year-on-year, which was the continuation of the downward trend since 2010. Brazil, Russia, India and South Africa's economic growth rate were 0.1 percent, 0.6 percent, 5.8 percent and 1.4 percent respectively[2]. Among the emerging market economies, Brazil was plagued by high inflation. Its industrial production has shrunken for over 8 months. And CPI grew by 6.41 percent[3]. As for Russia, due to geopolitical conflicts and sanctions by the West, its economy was badly affected by capital flight, the devaluation of the Ruble, growth slowdown and trade decline. As of end-2014, the exchange rate of Ruble against US Dollar fell about 40 percent compared with the year beginning. The annual CPI growth was 11.4 percent[4]. Indian economy started with a cyclical recovery. The inflation rate was on a downward trend. In December, the inflation rate was 5.86 percent. India's Prime Minister Narendra Modi carried out economic reforms, and made efforts to attract foreign investment. From May to September, foreign direct investment (FDI) in India was USD12.7 billion, an increase of 24 percent over the last year.

Thirdly, the international financial market saw intensified turbulence. There was an urgent need to strengthen coordination and cooperation among countries. Due to different pace of economic recovery, the landscape of global monetary policies became complicated and more difficult to coordinate. Meanwhile, the political and economic risks overlapped with increased volatility in international financial markets. In 2014, the stock markets in major developed countries witnessed ups and downs. The US Dow Jones, London FTSE 100 and Nikkei 225 closed at 17,823.07 points, 6,566.09 points, and 17,450.77 points, increasing by 7.25 percent, -2.17 percent, and 7.12 percent respectively over the year beginning.

Box 1   Progress in the international financial regulatory reform

In 2014, in accordance with working agenda, the Financial Stability Board (FSB) and Basel Committee on Banking Supervision (BCBS) continued to promote the international financial regulatory reform. Firstly, implementing the Basel III. In 2014, new progress was achieved in the formulation and implementation of international regulatory standards in Basel III. The announcement of revised program of the net stable funding ratio (NSFR) marked that harmonized quantitative regulatory standards on liquidity risk regulatory standards were established. So far, all 27 BCBS member jurisdictions launched and implemented the new capital rules. Most jurisdictions have issued the regulatory rules governing the liquidity coverage ratio, leverage ratio and systematically important banks.

Secondly, further improving the Basel regulatory framework. The BCBS came up with a series of proposals for improving the consistency and comparability of capital adequacy ratio (CAR), so as to maintain the international standard risk sensitivity to a certain degree, while reducing the complexity and enhancing the comparability and operation. First was to improve the regulatory rules. The capital requirement based on standard approach was the capital floor of advanced approach in avoidance of excessively lowering the capital requirement by internal model. Second was to enhance the disclosure requirement. This was to improve the consistency of risk measurement and capital adequacy ratio

---

① In 2013, capital outflows were USD15.9 billion.

② The International Monetary Fund, *World Economic Outlook*, January 2015.

③ Brazilian Institute of Geography and Statistics, January 2015.

④ Rosstat, January 2015.

information in the disclosure. Third was to sustain monitoring differences. It was to compare the capital requirement consequence with different model measurements on the same asset portfolio, analyze the cause and mitigate the difference. In 2014, BCBS released a series of international standards such as the supervision framework of the large risk exposure, capital requirements for bank exposures to central counterparties, the simple measurement approach for counterparty credit risk, capital requirements for bank to fund investment in the public entity, and capital measurement for asset securitization.

Thirdly, improving the risk control capability. In 2014, based on the experience and lessons in the international risk governance assessment, the FSC released a series of principles and guidelines to improve the risk control capability in banking sector, including the principles for effective risk appetite framework, the guideline for financial institutions to enhance risk culture, and it also released a survey report on implementation of sound compensation principles in some countries. The BCBS released the guideline on basic elements of capital planning procedure, the regulatory guideline on the identification and disposal of problem banks, and the guideline on improving the effectiveness of supervisory college in facilitating the cross-border and cross-sector regulatory cooperation. In addition, the BCBS revised and amended the guiding principle for strengthening bank corporate governance and issued the survey report on international banking sector's implementation of operational risk principle.

Fourthly, solving the "too-big-to-fail" problem. According to the requirement of G20 leaders, the FSB focused on properly assessing the systemic importance of the financial institutions, enhancing the capability of loss absorbency, increasing the regulatory intensity, and optimizing recovery and resolution plans. First is to identify the global systematically important financial institutions (G-SIFIs). In line with the 2013 year-end statistics, 30 global systematically important banks (G-SIB) were identified by BCBS, including 8 in the United States, 4 in France, 4 in Britain, 3 in China, 3 in Japan, 2 in Switzerland, 2 in Spain, 1 in Germany, Italy, Holland and Sweden respectively. The 30 G-SIBs should set aside 1 percent to 2.5 percent capital surcharge in accordance with their global systemic importance. Second is , to improve the total loss absotercy capability (TLAC). The G-SIBs were required to convert some or all bank debts into common equity or launch write-offs so that the creditors could bail-in themselves in case of failures instead of relying on government bailout. According to the proposal referred to public for comments, the minimum standard of TLAC including capital was set up in line with the QIS result in 2015. Yet this standard was not applicable to G-SIBs headquartered in emerging market countries at the preliminary stage. Third is to strengthen the regulatory intensity. Higher regulatory requirement was put forward in terms of risk appetite building, risk culture cultivation and risk identification and management while increasing the stress test requirement on the G-SIBs and paying close attention to the loss and capital gap under the extreme stress conditions. The FSB issued the *Key Attributes of Effective Resolution Regimes for Financial Institutions*, where the key points of resolution regimes for G-SIBs were put forward. These key points were improved in the revised version in October, 2014.

Fifthly, improving the supervision on shadow banking activities. The FSB suggested that regulatory authorities should intensify the information sharing and that the shadow banks were classified in accordance with five economic functions and different monitoring standards. These five economic functions include: a collection of investment (such as securities investment funds, hedge funds, private equity funds, trust investment institutions), issuing loans funded by short-term wholesale financing (for example, financial companies, financial leasing company, factoring companies, consumer credit institutions), securities brokers (securities dealers, the financing securities loan companies, money brokerage company), financing guarantee (guarantee companies, mortgage insurance institutions), asset securitization (related entities).

Sixthly, facilitating the financial infrastructure. The FSB made progress in enhancing the over-the – counter (OTC) derivatives markets (unified legal entity identifier (LEI), contract standardization, intensifying central counterparties (CCPs)), reducing reliance on rating agencies (reducing external ratings quotation, encourage institutions to strengthen their own credit risk assessment instead of external ratings), and reforming financial benchmark interest rate formation mechanism (solving the defects in LIBOR system).

2. Domestic economic and financial developments

In 2014, Chinese economy maintained overall stability within a proper range of growth while at the same time securing progress in its economic development in the new normal; agriculture witnessed a good harvest and industrial production registered steady growth. CPI remained stable and residents' income continued to increase. Economic restructuring made positive progress.

Firstly, domestic economy enjoyed steady performance. Through preliminary calculation, China's GDP recorded RMB63.65 trillion, up 7.4 percent year-on-year. Agriculture witnessed a good situation. Grain output exceeded 600 million kilos for 2 years, increasing for eleventh consecutive year. From January to December, the value added of large industrial enterprises increased by 8.3 percent year-on-year. Total urban fixed assets investment (excluding rural households) registered a nominal year-on-year increase of 15.7 percent. Retail sales of consumer goods went up 12.0 percent. The total imports and exports (USD) rose by 3.4 percent. CPI grew by 2.0 percent.

Secondly, economic structural adjustment showed positive progress. Strategic emerging industries maintained rapid growth. The new generation information technologies such as mobile internet, big data and cloud computing accelerated the integration with traditional industries. In 2014, the service industry increased by 8.1 percent, 0.8 percentage point higher than that of the secondary industry. Adjustment was promoted in the overcapacity industry with stronger pollution prevention and control. The main pollutants, particularly nitrogen oxide emissions decreased significantly. The unit GDP energy consumption fell by 4.8 percent year-on-year.

Thirdly, China continued to implement proactive fiscal policy and prudent monetary policy. In 2014, China's fiscal revenue stood at RMB14.04 trillion, up 8.6 percent year-on-year; total government expenditure was RMB15.17 trillion, up 8.2 percent over last year. Credit extension experienced a steady growth. M2 stood at RMB122.84 trillion at the end of December, up 12.2 percent year-on-year. While maintaining the continuity and stability of macroeconomic policies, China actively innovated the mentality and methodology of macro-control, fine-tuned the economy accordingly, and supported the service industry and micro and small-sized enterprises' development by directional tax reliefs such as expanding the scale of "replacing business tax with value-added tax (VAT)". Such regulatory policies as directional RRR cuts, refinancing, rediscounting and adjusting LTV ratio were taken, together with the issuance of special financial bonds to better support the real economy.

Fourthly, China's financial market maintained a steady growth on a whole. In 2014, China's stock market trading volume witnessed a significant growth and the market vigor was renewed remarkably. The main stock market index rose up; the scale of bond issuance was expanded and the direct financing function was well played. As of the end of December, Shanghai Composite Index closed at 3,234.68 points, 52.87 percent higher than the beginning of the year. The number of companies listed on the Shanghai Stock Exchange and Shenzhen Stock Exchange amounted to 2,613, with aggregated market value of RMB37.25 trillion. The annual aggregated amount of financing (including IPO, SEOs, right issue) was RMB485.643 billion. The aggregate value of bond issuance stood at RMB 11.0 trillion, an increase of 22.3 percent over the last year.

II. Latest development of China's banking sector

As of end-2014, China's banking sector consisted 3 policy banks, 5 large commercial banks, 12 joint-stock commercial banks, 133 city commercial banks, 665 rural commercial banks, 89 rural cooperative banks, 1,596 rural credit cooperatives (RCCs), 1 postal savings banks, 4 banking assets management companies, 41 locally incorporated foreign banking institutions, 1 China-German bausparkasse, 68 trust companies, 196 finance companies of corporate groups, 30 financial leasing companies, 5 money brokerage firms, 18 auto financing companies, 6 consumer finance companies, 1,153 village or township banks, 14 lending companies and 49 rural mutual cooperatives. In 2014, 5 private banks was approved to prepare for establishment with 1 opening business; 1 Trust Protection Fund was established. Overall, the number of incorporated banking institutions in China amounted to 4,091 with 3.76 million employees[1].

1. Banking assets

By the end of 2014, the total assets of China's banking sector increased by RMB21.0 trillion or 13.9 percent on a year-on-year basis to RMB172.3 trillion; the total liabilities rose by RMB18.8 trillion or 13.3 percent year-on-year to RMB160.0 trillion (see Chart 1). In terms of assets, large commercial banks, joint-stock commercial banks, and small- and medium-sized rural financial institutions plus the postal savings bank accounted for 41.2 percent, 18.2 percent and 16.5 percent respectively (see Chart 2).

Chart 1   Total assets and liabilities of banking institutions (2003-2014)

Unit: RMB trillion

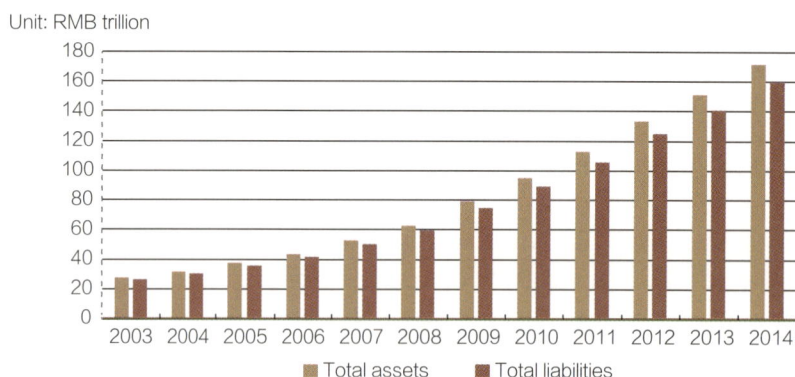

■ Total assets   ■ Total liabilities

Chart 2   Market share (by assets) of banking institutions (2003-2014)

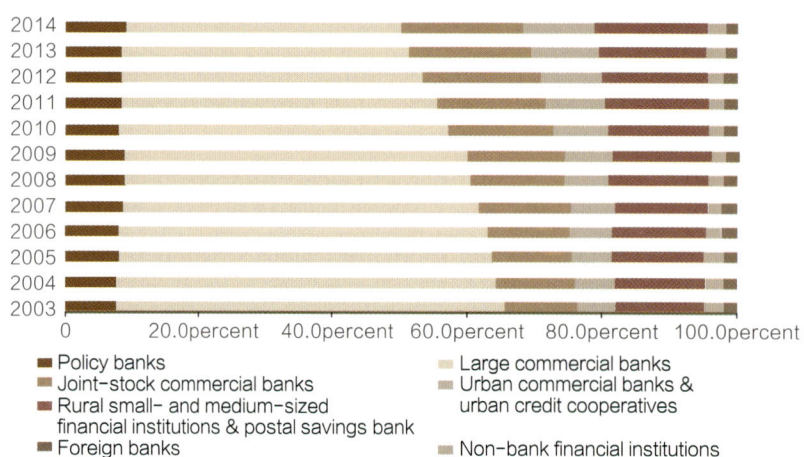

■ Policy banks
■ Joint-stock commercial banks
■ Rural small- and medium-sized financial institutions & postal savings bank
■ Foreign banks

■ Large commercial banks
■ Urban commercial banks & urban credit cooperatives

■ Non-bank financial institutions

---

[1] The private bank already opened and the Trust Protection Fund established are included in the total number of China's banking institutions and their number of employees are also included. But other statistics in this annual report exclude the above two institutions.

2. Bank deposits and loans

As of end-2014, the outstanding balance of deposits maintained by banking institutions increased by RMB10.2 trillion from the year beginning or 9.6 percent year-on-year to RMB117.4 trillion, among which the year-end household savings deposits grew by RMB3.8 trillion from year beginning or 8.4 percent year-on-year to RMB49.0 trillion; the corporate deposits rose by RMB4.9 trillion from year beginning or 9.1 percent year-on-year to RMB59.1 trillion. The outstanding balance of loans maintained by banking institutions went up RMB10.2 trillion from the year beginning or 13.3 percent year-on-year to RMB86.8 trillion. Short-term loans grew by RMB2.5 trillion from the year beginning or 7.9 percent year-on-year to RMB33.6 trillion; medium-to-long-term loans rose by RMB6.1 trillion from the year beginning or 15.0 percent year-on-year to RMB47.2 trillion; consumer loans increased by RMB2.4 trillion from the year beginning or 18.4 percent year-on-year to RMB15.4 trillion; bill financing increased by RMB961.6 billion from the year beginning or 49.0 percent year-on-year to RMB2.9 trillion (see Chart 3).

Chart 3   Deposits, loans & loan-to-deposit ratio (2003-2014)

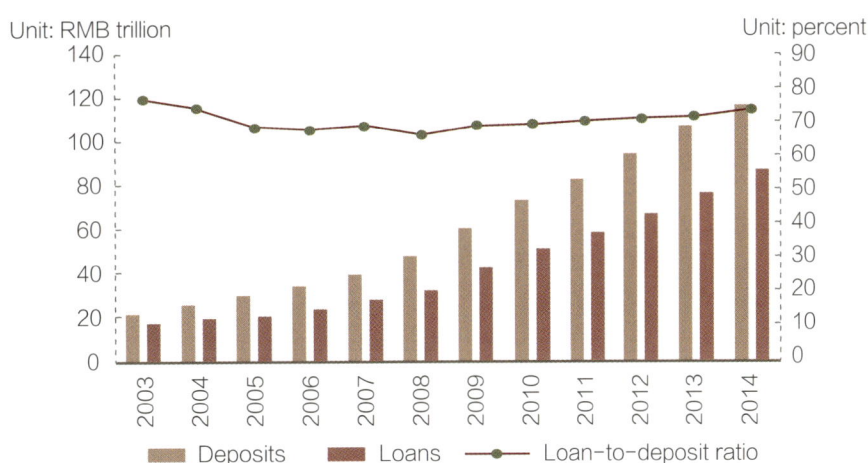

3. Capital Adequacy Ratio (CAR)

Since 2013, China's commercial banks implemented the *Capital Rules for Commercial Banks (Provisional)*. By the end of 2014, the Common Equity Tier 1 (CET1) capital adequacy ratio (CAR) of commercial banks was 10.56 percent, an increase of 0.61 percentage point from the year beginning; the tier 1 capital adequacy ratio (CAR) was 10.76 percent, an increase of 0.81 percentage point from the year beginning; the CAR was 13.18 percent, an increase of 0.99 percentage point from the year beginning.

4. Asset quality

In 2014, the newly added loans of banking institutions in the mainland of China were dominated by four sectors, though with concentration decreasing over previous year. The four sectors with highest proportions in the loans were namely personal loans (24.2 percent), real estate (13.4 percent), wholesale and retail (12.6 percent) and transportation, storage and postal industry (10.2 percent). The four sectors combined accounted to 60.4 percent of the total, a decrease of 7.3 percentage points over 2013. As of end-2014, the outstanding balance of NPLs in China's banking sector stood at RMB1.43 trillion, up RMB257.4 billion from the year beginning. The NPLs ratio of all banking institutions registered at 1.60 percent, up 0.11 percentage point year-on-year. With respect to commercial banks only, their NPLs rose to RMB842.6 billion, up RMB250.6 billion from the year beginning, and the NPLs ratio increased to 1.25 percent, up 0.25 percentage point year-on-year (see Chart 4).

Chart 4   NPL ratio of commercial banks (2007-2014)

Unit: percent

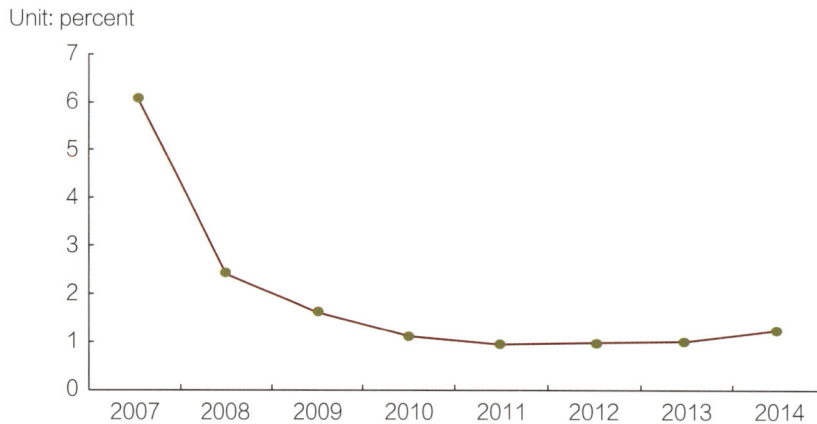

5. Risk-absorbing capability

As of end-2014, the loan loss provisions set aside by commercial banks increased by RMB281.3 billion from the year beginning to RMB1.96 trillion, while their provisioning coverage ratio dropped by 50.6 percentage points to 232.1 percent (see Chart 5). The provisioning ratio (provisions against total loans) reached 2.9 percent, up 0.07 percentage point year-on-year.

Chart 5   Asset impairment provisions and provisioning coverage ratio (2007-2014)

Unit: RMB 100 million   Unit: percent

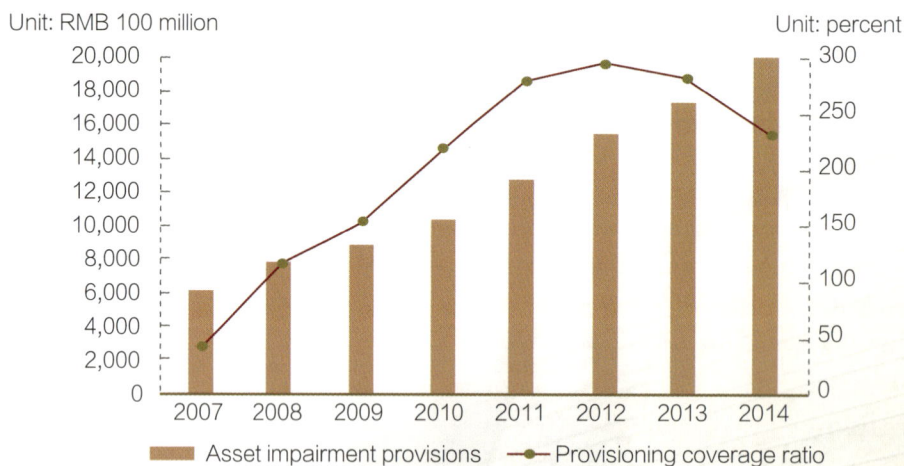

Asset impairment provisions   Provisioning coverage ratio

6. Net profitability

In 2014, banking institutions realized an after-tax profit of RMB1.93 trillion, representing a year-on-year increase of 10.5 percent. The Return on Equity (ROE) went down by 1.37 percentage points year-on-year to 17.1 percent, while the Return on Asset (ROA) stood at 1.19 percent, down by 0.03

percentage point year-on-year. The after-tax profit of commercial banks amounted to RMB1.55 trillion, up 9.7 percent year-on-year, with the ROE and ROA dropping by 1.58 percentage points and 0.04 percentage point year-on-year to 17.6 percent and 1.23 percent respectively (see Chart 6).

Chart 6   Income structure of banking institutions (2014)

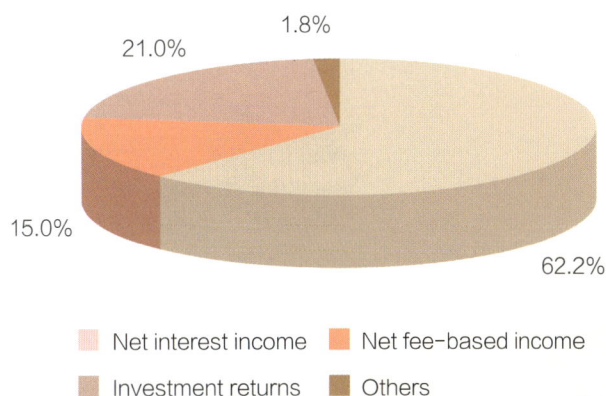

1.8%

21.0%

15.0%

62.2%

Net interest income   Net fee–based income

Investment returns   Others

7. Liquidity

As of end-2014, the average liquidity ratio of commercial banks increased by 2.42 percentage points year-on-year to 46.4 percent (see Chart 7); The RMB loan-to–deposit ratio was 65.1 percent. The RMB-denominated excess reserve ratio rose by 0.11 percentage point year-on-year to 2.65 percent.

Chart 7   Liquidity condition of banking institutions (January to December 2014)

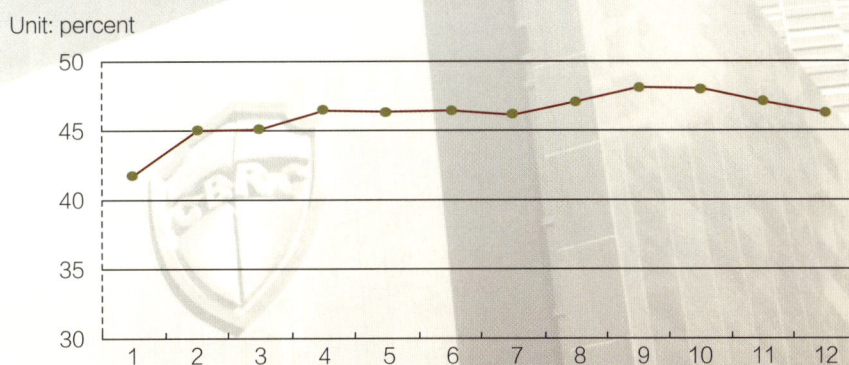

Unit: percent

Part Two

Banking Reform and Development

- Reform and transformation of the banking sector
- Financial Innovation
- Opening-up

The overall objective of banking reform and development is to establish "five systems": a system of banking institutions with wide-coverage of services, diversification of strategies and high efficiency; a banking service system responding to market demands and rooted in real economy; an operational and management system with better risk control and efficiency for banks; a stable and prudent regulatory system; and a coordinated financial market system that serves the real economy.

I. Reform and transformation of the banking sector

2014 was the year marking the beginning of comprehensively deepening reform. The CBRC set up a leading group and established the working mechanism and implementation planning to coordinately promote the banking reform. In 2014, the banking system of governance reform went well. The policy bank reform has made new progress. And new breakthrough was achieved in private capital participating in the banking sector.

1. Governance system reform

In 2014, the CBRC proposed to improve the banking governance, market system and regulatory system, and promote the modernization of banking governance capability. The focus was to improve corporate governance, business governance, risk governance, and industry governance.

Firstly, reform the corporate governance system. The CBRC continued to urge banking institutions to further perfect the governance structure and mechanism combining checks and balances and incentives of the general meeting of shareholders, board of directors, boards of supervisors and senior management, improve the performance assessment methods, establish a correct outlook on development, and gradually get rid of the inertial thinking of pursuing large scales, high performance indicators and high profits. The CBRC issued the *Rules on Supervision of Financial Asset Management Companies, Guiding Opinions on Strengthening Village banks Corporate Governance, Guidelines on Strengthening the Supervision over Commercial Banks' Development of the Mechanism for Providing Financial Services to Agriculture, Rural Areas and Farmers.*

Secondly, reform the business governance system. The CBRC endeavered to promote the banking institutions to adapt to banking group development and carry out reforms featuring subsidiary model business line model, SBU model and branch model in accordance with different business characteristics. All major commercial banks have established interbank business unit. Most banks with wealth management business have set up divisional organization for wealth management. The CBRC issued *Notice on Issues Related to Improving the Organization and Management System of Wealth Management Business of Banks* and the *Notice of the CBRC General Office on Regulating Interbank Business of Commercial Banks.*

Box 2   Improving interbank business and wealth management business governance

On April 24, 2014, the CBRC, the People's Bank of China (PBC), China Securities Regulatory Commission (CSRC), China Insurance Regulatory Commission (CIRC), and the State Administration of Foreign Exchange (SAFE) jointly issued the *Notice on Standardizing Inter-bank Businesses of Financial Institutions* (CBRC [2014] 127). The Notice required the banking institutions to standardize the interbank business activities, effectively prevent and control risks, and guide capitals flowing into real economy. In May, the *Notice of the CBRC General Office on Regulating Interbank Business of Commercial Banks* was issued, which reinforced the requirement for banking institutions to strengthen management, control risks, and return to their nature in order to strengthen interbank business governance. In October, the CBRC issued the *Notice on Conducting Special Inspections over the Implementation of New Inter-bank Regulations by Banking Institutions*. The Notice required banking institutions to inspect their own implementation of new interbank regulations. The CBRC also conducted onsite inspections.

To optimize the bank's wealth management business management system and standardize the development, in July, the CBRC issued *Notice on Issues Related to Improving the Organization and Management System of Wealth Management Business of Banks*. The Notice required that the banking institutions should improve the internal management system of wealth management businesses, set up wealth management business department responsible for dealing with wealth management businesses of the whole bank. Banks must meet the four basic requirements of "separate accounting, risk isolation, code of conduct and centralized management by specified departments" in dealing with wealth management business to prevent risk accumulation and return to the nature of asset management. By the end of 2014, most of banking institutions in dealing with wealth management business completed the SBU reform of wealth management. 525 banking institutions offered 54,107 types of wealth management products, with a total book balance of RMB15.03 trillion, an increase of 47.16 percent by the end of 2013.

Media perspective 1   To open the "right door" for interbank business, new regulations push ahead the financial service industry

A total of 5 agencies including PBC and CBRC jointly issued the *Notice on Standardizing Inter-bank Businesses of Financial Institutions* (hereinafter referred to as the "Notice") in May, 2014. The notice further standardized the interbank business operations of financial institutions.

Interbank business refers to all kinds of businesses conducted by financial institutions established according to laws within the territories of the People's Republic of China, with investment and finance as the core businesses, mainly including inter-bank lending, inter-bank deposits, inter-bank borrowing, inter-bank payments and buying securities for re-sales (selling securities for re-purchases).

In recent years, China's inter-bank businesses of financial institutions have witnessed rapid growth, playing a significant role in facilitating liquidity management, optimizing allocation of financial resources, and serving the real economy. Data show that from early 2009 to the end of 2013, the interbank assets booked as inter-bank deposits, inter-bank lending and securities buying for re-sales increased from RMB6.21 trillion to RMB21.47 trillion, a growth of 246 percent, which was 1.79 times and 1.73 times more than the total assets and loan growth respectively over the same period. However, the deputy director of the PBC Financial Stability Bureau Liang Shidong said that at present, there still exist some problems such as lack of standardization in some of business operations, inadequate information disclosure, and evading financial supervision and macro-control.

On the premise of supporting financial innovations and safeguarding independent operations of financial institutions, with the guideline of "blocking astray, opening right door, strengthening management, and promoting development", the Notice has put forward 18 guiding opinions concerning issues such as the standardization of inter-bank business operations of financial institutions, enhancement and improvement in the internal and external management of inter-bank businesses, and promotion of standard assets and liabilities business innovation activities.

 "Considering the large scale of interbank business, the stock business will be naturally settled with non-retroactivity". The Notice standardizes the scale of interbank businesses of financial institutions for the first time, stipulating that the balance of interbank investment for a commercial bank shall not exceed one third of the total liabilities of the bank. But the rural credit union, provincial incorporated PCC, and village banks are excluded temporarily.

Meanwhile, the Notice supported financial institutions to accelerate the normalized development of asset securitization. Financial institutions should actively participate in the pilot program of inter-bank deposits business in the inter-bank market and improve the initiative, standardization and transparency of assets and liabilities management.

"I hope the interbank business back to its origin rather than being the risk sources", Liang said. Although there is no existence of the empty operation of the funds, some interbank businesses actually elongate the capital chain. And each link in the chain produces certain cost. The Notice including a series of stipulations is favorable for guiding more capital into real economy, lowering enterprises financing cost, and improving financial institutions capability to support real economy.

In addition, the CBRC also issued the ***Notice of the CBRC General Office on Regulating Interbank Business of Commercial Banks*** (Yin Jian Fa [2014] 140). As the supporting policy document of the Notice on Standardizing Inter-bank Businesses of Financial Institutions, "No.140"clearly points out that except the SBU of commercial banks, other departments and branches may not operate interbank business.

(Source: Economic Daily, Reporters: Zhang Chen, Chen Guojing)

Thirdly, reform risk governance system. On the basis of consolidating and strengthening banking institutions credit risk control mechanism, in accordance with the facts that the off-balance sheet activities developed rapidly, banking group management trend was evident, the pace of "going global" was accelerating, the CBRC enhanced the comprehensive risk management

During 2014 Chinese New Year Holiday, the CBRC Chairman SHANG Fulin made a field trip to an ABC outlet.

system of on- and off-balance sheet activities, domestic and overseas market, local- and foreign-currency denominated business, parent and subsidiaries entities at a group level. According to the principal of substance over form, the CBRC established systems such as the full aperture and different levels capital calculation and risk provision system covering non-credit asset and off-balance sheet asset, meanwhile strengthened the main responsibility for risk governance at a group level, and further clarified the supervision responsibility for regulatory institutions. The CBRC issued the ***Guidelines on Consolidated Management and Supervision of Commercial Banks, Rules on Liquidity Risk Management of Commercial Banks (Trial), Notice of CBRC on Issuing the Guidelines on Supervisory Ratings of Commercial Banks.***

Fourthly, reform the industry governance system. On the basis of the consolidation of industry self-regulatory mechanism, the CBRC continued to intensify the service and rescue capabilities. On one hand, in light of banks management and actual development, the CBRC quickened the building of industry organization. On the other hand, through the industry association, the CBRC accelerated the infrastructure building, for instance, the related product information registeration system, laying foundation for increasing transparency and enhancing market oversight. According to risk control requirement, the CBRC timely promoted the institutional building within the industry and further maintained industry stability. The CBRC and the Ministry of Finance issued the **Rules for the Administration of the Trust Protection Fund** (CBRC [2014] 50). Hence, the China Trust Protection Fund was founded on December 19.

2. Institutional reforms

(1)The CDB and policy banks

The policy banks clarified their function orientations, with well coordinated policy business and market-oriented operations, that were subjects standardized supervision. In 2014, the China Development Bank (CDB) carried out in-depth reform and had an important bearing on serving national strategy and real economy. The CDB set up the housing finance division to better fund the nationwide renovation of shanty neighborhoods. By the end of 2014, the CDB accumulatively granted RMB806.9 billion in loans to help redevelop shanty households, of which in 2014 the amount was RMB408.6 billion, with a wide coverage of over 30 provinces(autonomous regions and municipalities), benefiting nearly 9.16 million households. The overall reform program of Agricultural Development Bank of China (ADBC) was approved by the State Council, which clarified the overall objectives and key measures of the reform and urged ADBC to play an active role in rural financial system. The CBRC studied the reform program of the Export-Import Bank of China, improved its restraint mechanism, and called for increased support for bilateral and multilateral trade cooperation and enterprises' "going global".

(2)Large commercial banks

In 2014, large commercial banks continued to improve corporate governance, strengthen the capacity building and enhance the performance assessment mechanisms. They pushed steady reforms in SBU and franchising departments, etc., and made achivement in reengineering and transforming wealth management and interbank business development. They improved consolidated management framework through the establishment of a wide-coverage, multi-dimensional risk control mechanism, covering both on- and off- balance sheet activities, domestic and overseas markets, local- and foreign-currency denominated businesses, parent and subsidiaries entities, and enhanced their comprehensive risk management framework at the group level. Large commercial banks also enhanced the implementation of advanced measures under capital management, improved capital planning, conducted interal assessment of capital management and innovated capital tools. The development of crisis management mechanism and recovery & resolution plan (RRP) of global systematically important banks was also well under way. In line with their own circumstances such as client base and products, and through such means as organic growth and M&A. they further optimized the layout of their overseas establishments and made steady progress in internationalized development.

(3)Small- and medium-sized commercial banks

In 2014, the small- and medium-sized commercials banks achieved development with the theme of "reform, innovation, better quality and risk control", with optimizing governance mechanism as their breakthrough, serving real economy as their mandate, and controlling risks as their bottom line, complying laws and regulations as their foundation, and constantly enhanced scientific management and sustainable development capability. They set up service network for MSE sub-branches and community sub-branches. In the context of deepening financial reform and new trend of wide application of network information technology such as internet, mobile devices and big data, the small- and medium-sized commercials banks, innovated their products, services and channels, improved service quality, lowered service cost, and standardized service pricing. On the premise of enhancing consolidated supervision and risk isolation, some qualified small- and medium-sized commercials banks formulated their own development strategy and market orientation and prudently conducted cross-sector operations. The CBRC improved business governance, encouraged small- and medium-sized commercials banks to innovate business governance and realize the transformation from "department-based bank" to "process-based bank".

Thematic column 1   Private capital participating in the banking sector

The CBRC adhered to the principle of fairness and equal treatment to all forms of capital, including private capital, in their investment in the banking sector. There were no additional legal or regulatory barriers or preconditions inhibiting the flow of private capital into banking institutions. In terms of market entry, private capital flowed to the banking sector through participating in new entities establishment, new shares subscription, equity purchase, and mergers & acquisitions. At present, more than 100 small- and medium-sized commercial banks had over 50 percent private capital in their capital composition, some of which were even 100 percent privately funded. The rural cooperative banking institutions had over 90 percent private capital in their capital composition, and the village banks had over 72 percent private capital in their capital composition.

Since 2014, the CBRC launched the first pilot project of private banks, and came up with some framework proposals approved by the State Council. The current pilot has achieved initial results. In March 2014, the CBRC released the first batch of five private banks on a trial basis approved by the State Council, officially launching the pilot program of private banks. Under the principle of voluntariness and sustainability, the CBRC actively collaborated with the main institutions to improve their establishment plans.

The pilot selection considered five factors: first,

there was institutional arrangement for bearing the remaining risks; second, having the qualifications to run a bank and ability to resist risks; third, the shareholders accepted supervision; fourth, there was differentiated market orientation and specific strategies; fifth, having legal and feasible recovery and resolution plan. The first batch of five private banks on a trial basis showed the features of serving micro, small, and medium-enterprises, "three rural issues", and communities. Among them, Tianjin Jincheng Bank focused on the business of "corporate deposit and loan", Zhejiang Wangshang Bank highlighted the business of "small deposit and loan", Shenzhen Qianhai Weizhong Bank implemented "retail deposit and small loan" policy, and Shanghai Huarui Bank and Wenzhou Minshang Bank insisted on "specific area" business models.

In July, 2014, the CBRC approved the application for establishment of Shenzhen Qianhai Weizhong Bank (also known as WeBank), Wenzhou Minshang Bank and Tianjin Jincheng Bank. In September, the CBRC approved the application for establishment of Shanghai Huarui Bank and Zhejiang Wangshang Bank. And Shenzhen Qianhai Weizhong Bank and Shanghai Huarui Bank were approved to open business in December, 2014 and January, 2015 respectively.

In 2014, the CBRC issued the **Rules on Implementation**

of Administrative Licensing Items for Rural Small- and Medium-sized Banking Institutions and the *Notice on Encouraging and Guiding Private Capital to Participate in Ownership Reform of Rural Credit Cooperatives.* The CBRC supported private capital participating in the establishment of rural medium- and small-sized banking institutions and encouraged all private investors, especially private enterprises dealing with agricultural businesses, to participate in the ownership reform of rural credit cooperatives and in the capital expansion of rural commercial banks. By the end of 2014, private capital accounted for 88percent stake in the small- and medium-sized rural financial institutions, an increase of 0.3 percentage point over the beginning of the year.

In 2014, the CBRC guided and standardized all ownership capital in the participation of non-banking institutions. On January 1st, the newly revised *Administrative Rules on the Pilot Program of Consumer Finance Companies* (hereinafter referred to as "measures") became effective. The Rules defined that domestic non-financial companies with a certain level of financial strength whose products are fit for consumer finance are allowed to become principal contributors of consumer finance companies. On March 13th, the CBRC revised and amended the *Rules Governing Financial Leasing Companies* (hereinafter referred to as the "Rules"). The Rules allowed the initiator-based model to replace the contributor-based model. The initiators that met the related requirements of the CBRC were admitted to establish financial leasing companies. 43 private holding non-banking institutions were opened, including 11 trust companies, 26 financial companies, 3 financial leasing companies , 2 auto finance companies, 1 consumer finance company, and 6 of them were newly established in 2014, including the 4 financial companies, 1 auto finance company and 1 consumer finance company. In addition, 11 private holding non-banking institutions were approved but did not open for business, including 5 finance companies, 2 financial leasing companies, 3 auto finance companies and 1 consumer finance company.

◎ WeBank was established in Qianhai, Shenzhen

On July 24, 2014, the first private bank, Shenzhen Qianhai WeBank Co., Ltd. was established with the approval from the CBRC. Guided by the mandate of promoting financial inclusion, WeBank focuses on providing quality and convenient financial services to retail clients such as urban white collars, industrial workers and migrant workers and micro and small corporate clients that meet with national industrial policies. The services include deposit taking, wealth management and investment, with the emphasis on personal credit loans, micro and small business loans and credit card business to foster the bank's brand in retail and small value businesses.

◎ Shanghai Huarui Bank

Shanghai Huarui Bank was established on September 26, 2014 with the approval from the CBRC. It opened business on January 27, 2015 after approved by the CBRC Shanghai Office. Shanghai Huarui Bank was incorporated in Shanghai Free Trade Zone (SFTZ) with a registered capital of RMB3 billion. As the first incorporated bank in SFTZ, Shanghai Huarui Bank endeavors to become a MSE-oriented bank that serve the financial needs of the general public.

◎ The CBRC Sichuan Office promoted private capital investment in City Commercial Banks and Rural Cooperatives

The CBRC Sichuan Office actively promoted private capital investment to participate in the equity reform of Rural Credit Cooperatives and restructuring of Rural Commercial Banks. In the process of reform, leading enterprises in agricultural industrialization, agricultural product processing and agricultural trade received preferred considerations to become shareholders so as to support the "Three Rural Issues" and foster long-term investment. As of end 2014, the shareholding ratio of private capital in Sichuan Rural Cooperative Organizations reached 92.96 percent. Capital replenish plan of City Commercial Banks was also steadily implemented. In 2014, 5 City Commercial Banks carried out the equity and capital supplement with a total of RMB1,568 million replenished. As of end 2014, the shareholding ratio of private capital in City Commercial Banks reached 57.42 percent.

Unit: percent

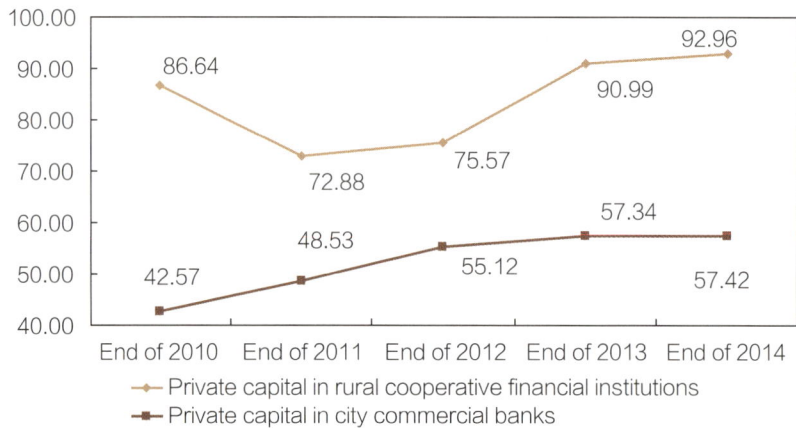

Private capital proportion of rural cooperative financial institutions and city commercial banks in Sichuan province

Media perspective 2   The first 5 private bank pilots program was selected, involving 10 private investors

The CBRC Chairman Shang Fulin said in an interview with China Daily, that after a comprehensive review and agreed by the state council, the first 5 private banks was selected from recommended pilot programs. The pilot will follow the principle of co-sponsors, which requires every pilot bank to have at least 2 initiators to carry out preparations and observe the shareholding ratio requirement on individual shareholders.

Next, the CBRC will strictly check qualifications of the initiators, and the formal application would be accepted if the capital is qualified. The CBRC will steadily push

CBRC Chairman SHANG Fulin: New breakthrough made in the co-sponsorship model of private banks.

forward the first group of pilot program. The pilot will be further expanded after gaining experience.

Host: Mr. Shang, can you tell us a little bit about the work process of private bank?

Shang Fulin: It is a very important content of banking reform for private banks to bear risks. In the banking sector, introducing competition mechanism could improve the service of the bank and enable banks to improve service quality. This work has been put in the list of reform projects in this year. After a comprehensive review and agreed by the state council, the first 5 private bank pilot program was selected from recommended pilot programs. The pilot will follow the principle of co-sponsors, which requires every pilot bank to have at least 2 initiators to carry out preparations and follow the rule of equity cap for sole shareholder. Next, the CBRC will strictly check qualifications of shareholders of the mentioned private investors, and the formal application would be accepted if the capital is qualified.

Host: How are these programs finally determined?

Shang Fulin: The program of pilot private bank that put forward by the Party central committee and the State Council received positive responses from private enterprises and local governments, . We have selected 5 pilots private banks program after a comprehensive screening of these programs recommended and reported by various regions. The selection of the 5 pilots is neither quota distribution under planned economy mode, nor regional distribution under administrative management, but optimal program from recommended pilot programs from across the nation. Major criteria include five factors:

Firstly, the bank should have a system to bear residual risk. We all know that bank needs to manage risks, and risk has the characteristic of spillover. It must be managed once they arise. Bank also needs to prevent the spillover of risk, and prevent risk from damaging the legitimate rights and interests of depositors.

Secondly, the bank should have risk control capability and qualifications to well manage the bank. For example, sufficient net capital, excellent main business and good track record.

Thirdly, the bank should have an agreement term that shareholders accept regulation.

Fourthly, the bank should have differentiated market positioning and specific strategies.

Fifthly, the bank should have legal and feasible risk recovery and resolution plan ("living wills").

The CBRC will steadily push forward the first group of pilot program. The pilot will be further expanded after gaining experience.

Host: Well, actually private bank is not a kind of new institutions. There are also many banks that absorbed private capital investment. But why we put forward the idea of the pilot?

Shang Fulin: Private capital is permitted to be invested in banks by law, and practice has proved that it has become very common in our daily life. The injection of private capital in banking sector mainly occurred in the process of the merger and reorganization and bank restructuring and transformation. There are very few banks that are established by private capital, and even less of them can really bear residual risk. Therefore, this pilot is mainly a test for new mechanisms to take risks.

Private bank should hold the bottom line of preventing and controlling risks.

Host: Mr. Li, What do you think of the significance of this five requirements in promoting private bank development?

Li Yang: Now the "glass door" that prevents the private capital from going into the financial sector has been removed, but we still need to focus on two questions: first, people have a misunderstanding over private capital banks. They feel that the banks are the same as general companies, and by owning banks, they can manipulate their financing. But actually, bank is a special industry; it is a franchise in any country and must have strict qualification examination and supervision. This is because bank is serving the public. Although equity is completely private, its business activities have externalities and it is public to a large extent. Therefore, there must be laws and institutions to safeguard public interests. The second is risk. This program has proposed risk bearing, in fact, it is emphasizing the decisive role of market. As the market allows you to engage in business, it also requires you to take risks when problems come.

Host: As the president of large bank, I wonder that what's your opinion upon the pilot private bank?

Zhang Hongli: Systemic risk is the main concern of banks, because if problems occur in one bank, there will be systemic effects, and we hope that both us and competitors can secure healthy growth. The bottom line of opening a private bank is to avoid any systemic risk, render service to the real sector, protect the interests of the consumers and ensure fair competition. In an open industry, each investor should carry out financial activities, accept supervision, and bear the same responsibilities and obligations in the same environment.

In my opinion, private bank may have in an inferior position in terms of credit; it may be difficult to absorb public deposits. To solve this problem, while building the private credit system, we should also establish risk bearing mechanism and deposit insurance system to protect the interests of the depositors and make the public have more confidence in private banks.

We have done a good job in the first step of deepening financial reform.

The first batch of pilot private banks have uncovered the mysterious veil of private bank that was invested by private capital. This marked the first step made in comprehensively deepening reform of banking.

The private bank pilot emphasizes differential positioning; it is not only the original intention to launch the pilot of private banks, but also a unique choice for private banks to adapt to the fierce competition in the market. Since the beginning of reform and development in China's banking industry, we are not in shortage of banks, let alone large banks. The problem is that we are short of small-sized banks that can service our community, MSEs and disadvantaged groups, and we are also short of products and services to meet the needs of our customers. But in fact, for a long time, be it big or small, all banks' operation mode are becoming similar, and they all pursue for large scales. This time private banks are bringing natural "genes" of folk capital into banks, which share inherent affinity with private enterprises. They have a better understanding of the requirements and characteristics of private enterprises, and they are also more willing to render service to small and medium-sized private enterprises, to find the weak spot of the market and bring its superiority into full play to serve the MSEs, community members and "agriculture, rural areas and farmers". Private banks with less capital and accumulations can only find opportunities to grow in these areas by blazing the development road with its own characteristics. Or it will be difficult for them to compete with big banks. With the establishment of private banks, more and more ordinary consumers will enjoy the convenient financial services, and the inclusive financial system will be more perfect.

Risk control is the lifeline of banks, for people who have no experience in running banks , risk prevention is more important. In this pilot program of private banks, the person who funded the establishment of the bank could benefit from it and shall also bear the corresponding risk. Therefore the banks are required to have the ability of taking risks; we should require the establishment of risk bearing responsibility system, improvement of the risk control mechanism and formulation of "living wills". During the whole process, there must be a corresponding mechanism in each link to ensure that the risk of bank would not trigger spillover. Effective control of risk is the key to the success of private bank.

Banks are the pillars of a country's finance. During the process of piloting banking reform, we should fight against the impacts of our mistakes and remember to avoid blind mass action. The pilot will be further expanded after gaining experience. The CBRC will steadily push forward the first group of pilot program. In this sense, the principle of "one by one" is particularly important. While at the same time relative supporting system are also needed. Let us wait patiently for private banks, a "catfish" that is established purely by private capital, and let us wait for them to inject new vigor and vitality into China's banking reform.

(Sources: People's Daily, Reporter: Ouyang Jie Excepts)

(4)Small-and Medium-sized rural banking institutions

In 2014, small-and medium-sized rural banking institutions have kept its sound development momentum by focusing on the main line of "preventing risks, promoting the reform, strengthening service". Throughout the year, 200 new rural commercial banks were newly built and the number of rural commercial banks has reached 725 in total. The assets, liabilities and owners' equity of rural commercial bank accounted for 58.5percent, 57.9 percent and 66.8 percent of rural cooperative financial institutions respectively. The establishment of village and township banks (VTB) are being done in a orderly way, with 162 VTBs newly built, making the number of newly built VTBs exceeding

150 for the past 4 consecutive years, and covering 54.6 percent of countries, of which 61.1 percent are located in the Midwest. The proportion of VTBs shareholding of private capital has reached 72.6 percent. Industry audit system of provincial credit unions was carried out in a orderly way, with capital business attaining normal development, function transformation gradually deepened, and service functions further strengthened. Strategic transformation is speeding up gradually. 17 rural and commercial bank have pioneered in carrying out the asset securitization and financial service, Qiongzhong Credit Union became the first banking institution to get lised on the new three board (OTC market for growth enterprises). Some basic rural financial services, including the project of "financial services to every village" have made solid progress, and agriculture loan balance of small and medium-sized rural financial institutions has reached RMB7.5 trillion, accounting for 67.4 percent of total loans.

(5)Postal Savings Bank of China

In 2014, the Postal Saving Bank of China continued to deepen the shareholding reform, which included kicking off the process of attracting strategic investors, improving its governance structure and accelerating the transformation to a modern commercial bank. It restructured the internal business departments and optimized business process in an orderly way, improved the internal audit system and set up regional auditing center to strengthen the audit independence and enhance internal controls. It organized recruitment event that gathered thousands of job-hunters in order to recruit experienced professionals. Focusing on rendering service to rural areas, community and small and medium-sized enterprises, the Bank constructed five cooperation platforms that linked banks with security companies, industrial associations, enterprises, guarantee companies and insurance companies, established featured MSE-oriented sub- branches, and intensified the efforts to serve the real economy.

(6)Financial asset management companies

In 2014, the financial asset management companies continued to promote the commercialization. China Cinda Asset Management Co., Ltd. further improved its corporate governance, business operations and information disclosure in accordance with the requirements for listed companies. China Huarong Asset Management Co., Ltd. has entered into cooperation with seven strategic investors to further strengthen its capital strength and optimize the equity structure. The China Great Wall Asset Management Corporation, China Orient Asset Management Corporation accelerated their shareholding reform and improved corporate governance. To improve supervision on the diversified developments of financial asset management companies, the CBRC, the Ministry of Finance (MOF), the People's Bank of China (PBC), the China Securities Regulatory Commission (CSRC) and the China Insurance Regulatory Commission (CIRC) jointly issued the *Rules Governing Financial Asset Management Companies* (hereinafter referred to as the Rules). The **Rules** covered corporate governance, risk management, management of internal transaction, special purpose entities, capital adequacy, financial soundness, information resources and information disclosure, etc., for the purpose of strengthening the supervision of financial asset management companies at the group level after its reform and transformation, and promoting the risk control capacity of the group to secure prudent operation and healthy development.

(7)Trust companies

In accordance with the principle of "well managing the entrusted money", trust companies further broadened the market dimensions of assets and wealth management, thus, diversifying the means to increase the value of entrusted properties. At the same time, substantial breakthroughs have been made in the institutional building and overarching mechanism construction. The CBRC drafted the *Regulations governing the Trust Company*, which regulate the operations and conducts of trust companies, protect the rights and interests of trustees and the public, strengthen the supervision and management of trust companies and promote the healthy development of the trust sector. The CBRC adjusted the net capital calculation criteria and established a reasonable and clear measurement method for classifying capital, distinguished between transaction management business from propietary management business, and strengthened capital constraints of credit-linked trust business. It revised the *Guidelines of Regulatory Rating and Classification Supervision*, linking the rating results to the business scope, gradually realizing the limited-license-based supervision. The CBRC drafted the *Administrative Measures for Trust Registration*, promoted the development of trust products registration system for product registration, launch, disclosure and trading. It required the establishment of recovery and resolution mechanism by trust companies so as to enhance shareholders' responsibility and their risk control capacity. It issued the *Guiding Opinions for the Risk-based Supervision of Trust Companies* to setting out the directions for risk prevention, strategic transformation and scientific supervision of trust companies. In 2014, the *Rules for the Administration of the Trust Protection Fund* and *the Supervisory Measures governing China Trust Protection Fund Company Limited* became effective, which set up the China Trust Protection Fund Company Limited, an industrial stabilization mechanism for maintaining the safety and soundness of the financial market.

As of end-2014, there were 68 trust companies with assets under management (AUM) reaching RMB13.98 trillion, operating 37,762 trust projects and realizing investment profits of RMB483.1 billion.

Box 3　Creation of the Trust Protection Fund

On December 19, the China Trust Protection Fund Co., Ltd. (CTPF) was founded at the 2014 Annual Conference of China's Trust Industry.

The establishment of the Company was approved by the State Council and the CBRC, and the CTPF is subject to supervision of the CBRC. The CTPF is funded by the China Trustee Association along with 13 trust companies.

As the manager of the protection funds, the CTPF is responsible for the raising, managing and using of the funds and for running financial businesses approved by the supervisory authorities. Instead of pursuing profits, the CTPF regards the management of the protection funds as its main responsibility and takes risk mitigation and resolution of the trust industry as a top priority. Subject to the supervision of the CBRC, the CTPF must meet the requirements on capital adequacy, liquidity ratio and other core indicators. The CTPF shall establish and improve the modern corporate governance structure in accordance with the *Company Law*, with the shareholders' meeting, board of directors, supervisory board and management fulfilling their respective functions pursuant to applicable laws and regulations. It shall set up sound operation and management rules and risk control system in accordance with the *Rules for the Administration of the China Trust Protection Found Company Limited* so as to ensure sound and stable operation of the Company.

The CTPF will follow the market approach, and its establishment will make the protection funds more resilient, thus ensuring better risk mitigation and resolution. Consequently, the investors will become more confident and the development of the trust sector will be promoted. At the same time, such an institutional design marks an active effort to enhance China's financial stability as well as an innovative practice in reforming the institutional arrangements for the safety net.

Media perspective 3   The promulgation of the *Rules for the Administration of the Trust Protection Fund* creates a "safety net" for the trust sector

When offering assistance to a trust company, the CTPF is required to follow the market approach. The assistance is neither a cost-free one nor a reverse incentive for the trust company and its shareholders.

In principle, a four-step approach will be adopted in deal with the risks facing a trust company. The four steps are: debt restructuring, external takeover, execution of recovery and resolution plan, and utilization of protection funds.

China's trust sector is next to the banking sector in terms of assets under management. It has been growing very fast. Statistics show that as of the end of Q3 2014, the AUM of trust companies reached RMB12.95 trillion. However, risks have been emerging in the trust sector due to increased downward pressure on growth and buildup of excess capacity.

In order to safeguard the rights and interests of the parties in trust deals, effectively guard against trust risks, and promote the sustained and health growth of the trust sector, the CBRC has made and issued the **Rules for the Administration of the Trust Protection Fund** (the "Rules") jointly with the Ministry of Finance.

Adoption of the market approach

According to the **Rules**, the China Trust Protection Fund (the "Protection Fund') and the China Trust Protection Fund Company Limited (the "CTPF") will be created. The Protection Fund and the CTPF will be subject to the supervision of the CBRC.

As the manager of the Protection Fund, the CTPF is responsible for the raising, managing and using of the funds and for running financial businesses approved by the supervisory authorities. Instead of pursuing profits, the CTPF regards the management of the protection funds as its main responsibility and takes risk mitigation and resolution of the trust industry as a top priority. The investment of the Protection Fund is limited to low-risk and highly liquid products, such as bank deposits, government bonds, financial bonds, and etc..

The **Rules** specifies that in order to prevent moral hazard, the CTPF will adhere to the principle of "holding the seller accountable" and "letting the buyer beware" in dealing with risks in the trust sector, and the market-based mechanism will play a decisive role. When offering aid to a trust company, the CTPF is required to follow the market approach. The aid is neither a cost-free one nor a reverse incentive for the trust company and its shareholders. Once the Protection Fund steps in, original shareholders and executive officers of the trust company in question will be held to account. A market exit may be implemented when necessary.

Such an institutional arrangement will help to maintain the stability of the trust sector, ensure the "survival of the fittest" in accordance with market mechanism, properly address the "rigid payment" issue, and prevent trust companies and their shareholders from moral hazard, said a CBRC official.

Five assistance circumstances

As for raising further capital, the official said, unified criteria will be implemented for the subscription of the Protection Fund because the supervisory rating system applicable to trust companies is under revision. As the rating system becomes mature and well-established, differentiated subscription rules that reflect the risk level and profile of the trust companies will be implemented.

The official said that a four-step approach, namely "debt restructuring, external takeover, execution of the recovery and resolution plan, and employment of protection funds" will be adopted in dealing with risks facing a trust company. The Protection Fund will be the last resort to provide not-for-free aid for the trust company in trouble.

It is said that the Protection Fund will provide aid under the following five circumstances: 1) the trust company is insolvent and needs restructuring after the implementation of the recovery and resolution plan; 2) the trust company has kicked off the bankruptcy procedures in accordance with law and is being restructured; 3) the trust company has been ordered to close or revoked as a result of illegal operation; 4) the trust company needs short-term liquidity support due to temporary lack of working capital; 5) other circumstance under which there is a need to use the Protection Fund.

"Only under circumstance 4) can the CTPF decide whether to use the Protection Fund at its own discretion, provided the trust company in trouble makes the application, submits the liquidity issue solution and repayment plan, and signs a contract on the paid use of funds." Under the other circumstances, approval from the Fund's board of directors is required.

(Source: The Economic Daily. Journalist: Chang Yanjun)

◎ The CBRC Shaanxi Office drafted rules on risk classification and management of trust projects

The CBRC Shaanxi Office drafted rules for local trust companies to classify their valid trust projects into four risk tiers, including Pass, Special Mention, Abnormal and Problematic, and to manage them accordingly based on the correctness of the classification. To accomplish this, the companies should consider the migrations of the risk factors such as solvency of their counterparties, the volatility of the relevant collaterals and impawns and the variation on external situations.

(8)Finance companies of enterprise groups

In 2014, by focusing on the development of enterprise groups, the finance companies continued to play an active role in reducing costs, promoting product sales and supporting enterprises' strategic development. The CBRC and SASAC jointly issued the *Guidelines on Further Promoting the Sound Development of the Finance Companies of Central SOEs*, reiterating the basic orientation of finance companies and straightening out their management mechanisms so that large enterprise groups can work indirectly as a "ballast" of national economy in helping China react to economic periodic fluctuation effectively and realize sound and healthy development. The *Notice on Notifying Relevant Issues concerning the Supervision over Enterprise Group Finance Companies* was issued to promote the standardization and normalization of the supervision over finance companies. The *Guidelines for Rating of Enterprise Group Finance Companies* was drafted to build restraint mechanism for the development of finance companies. By the end of 2014, there were 196 enterprise group finance companies, with total on-and off-balance-sheet assets reaching RMB5.53 trillion. These finance companies provided services to approximately 45,000 member companies and the total assets of the enterprise groups exceeded RMB30 trillion.

(9)Financial leasing companies

In 2014, the CBRC issued the *Administrative Rules for Financial Leasing Companies* and formulated the *Provisional Rules on the Management of the Specialized Subsidiaries of Financial Leasing Companies*. The professionalization and core competitiveness of financial leasing companies was promoted steadily; the quality and efficiency of operation and development continued to improve. Asset portfolios of financial leasing companies have been further optimized, with the volume of direct leases and operating leases increasing year by year. By focusing on the combination of finance funds and assets, financial leasing companies have deepened the links in real economy industrial chain, playing an important role in supporting industrial upgrading, promoting the transformation of excess capacity, rendering service to MSEs as well as "Agriculture, Rural areas and Farmers" and other fields. By the end of 2014, there were 30 financial leasing companies, with total assets reaching RMB1.28 trillion and the net profit standing at RMB16.4 billion.

◎ The CBRC Tianjin Office is leading the financial leasing industry's innovative development

The CBRC Tianjin Office continually improved the mechanism of the industry and led the development. First of all, steadily strengthening the dominant position. The total assets scale of all financial leasing company within its jurisdiction accounted for 30 percent of the whole industry in China. Secondly, guiding the transformation to adapt to new market trend. It guided the industry to adjust business structure, revitalize stock assets, and utilize the flow of assets. The total assets of aircraft leasing exceeded RMB 63.1 billion. Container ship, offshore platform, high-end cruise leasing business have achieved breakthroughs; areas in energy saving and environmental protection, technical research were becoming new business growth points. Thirdly, supporting the exploration of specialized development path, and proactively promoting subsidiary to be set up within and out of China. Fourthly, promoting the innovation of funding channel.

(10)Auto finance companies

In 2014, the financial service and capacity of auto financing companies continued to improve, with diversified financing channels formed in this industry and sustainable development foundation further consolidated. By the end of 2014, personal auto loans accounted for 56.24 percent of all loans extended by banking institutions (not including the use of credit cards to pay for vehicle purchase by installments). In 2014, banks extended loans to auto dealers for financing 3.47 million vehicles in inventories and consumers for purchasing 2.25 million vehicles, thereby effectively boosting the consumption of vehicles and promoting the growth of the automotive industry.

(11)Consumer finance companies

In 2014, by focusing on meeting medium and low-income groups' demands of reasonable consumer credit, consumer finance companies continuously provided the market with more diversified credit products, explored cross-regional operation to expand their geographic presence and business coverage, and strengthened product and service innovation. The industry attained a sound development. In 2014, the first group of pilot banks, including Bank of Beijing Consumer Finance Co., Ltd., Bank of China Consumer Finance Co., Ltd., Home Credit Consumer Finance Co., Ltd. and Jincheng Consumer Finance Co., Ltd., extended 720,000 loans, each worth no more than RMB100,000, to consumers, accounting for 91 percent of all loans they extended. Of those, 450,000 loans were below RMB5,000, accounting for 57percent of all loans. These companies has became one of the important driving force of inclusive finance.

Box 4   Consumer finance companies boosted the consumption of low and medium-income groups

2014 marked the fourth year for China's pilot program of consumer finance companies. The functional orientation and profit model of consumer finance companies has become clearer, which has provided convenient consumer credit service for the majority of low and medium-income people, thereby improving people's living standard and helping them cultivate good credit concept. For example, Beijing

Consumer Finance extended education and training loans to students, blue-collar workers and white-collar employees to get further study. The Bank of China Consumer Finance developed a loan product called "easier credit, easier living", aiming to help college graduates pay their housing rent. Sichuan Jincheng Consumer Finance launched the "payroll loans" to meet the urgent spending needs of ordinary working-class. The Home Credit Consumer Financed worked constantly to meet young group's pursuit of fashionable life and the demands of basic necessary electric appliance of low-income families, especially some rural households.

(12) Currency brokerage companies

In 2014, the business volume and commission income of currency brokerage companies kept increasing at a high speed. With enhanced profitability and improved systems and services, currency brokerage companies continued to play a full role as "lubricants in financial markets". In 2014, there were 250,000 brokerage business transactions and 150,000 foreign exchange brokerage business transactions with the total value reaching RMB58 trillion and USD6 trillion respectively.

II.Financial innovation

The CBRC takes meeting the effective financial demand as both starting point and ultimate goal for innovation. Based on the principles of "controllable risks, calculable costs and sufficient information disclosure", the CBRC takes meeting actual demand of real economy and improving the banking competitiveness as the basic criteria for measuring the innovation. It promotes the banking innovation and development scientifically and prudentially while guarding against financial risks and maintaining financial stability, and thus promoting the sustainable and sound interaction between economy and finance.

In 2014, the banking industry made great efforts to strengthen the financial innovation and make innovation a new growth-driving engine. Firstly, banking institutions explored the use of information technologies to promote business innovation. They leverage the Internet, big data, cloud computing and other technical means to build the digital financial platform, consolidate the physical operation channels, and extend the virtual operation space. By optimizing and promoting online banking, telephone banking, cellphone banking and AMT self-service terminals, they kept diversifying the e-banking service channels, enlarging the coverage of services, extending the service time, and enhancing the service quality besides physical banking sites. Secondly, efforts were made to explore non-credit business innovation, develop businesses with high added value, such as wealth management, asset custody and so on. Thirdly, efforts were made to strengthen the innovation of liability business. Through financial bond, certificate of deposit, offer trading and other means, banking institutions raised funds and improved their active liability capacity. Fourthly, efforts were made to explore the credit business innovation and build new profit-making channels.

Box 5   Commercial banks commenced the pilot program of "direct financing tools for wealth management"

In recent years, banks' wealth management businesses have been playing a significant role in improving the social financing structure, supporting the development of real economy, meeting clients' demand in investment, increasing residents' property income and accelerating the transition of banking management. In order to promote the reasonable transition of wealth management business and provide better services for the real economy, the CBRC guided banking institutions to commence the pilot program of "direct financing tools for wealth management" (hereinafter referred to as "Tools") and "wealth management plans" (hereinafter referred to as "Plan") in October 2013. The "Tools" and "Plan" constituted a mechanism linking the supply of capital with the demand of capital. As a result, the goal of "reducing channels, shortening the chain and deleveraging" was achieved. In this way, the financing cost for enterprises was reduced, the capital use efficiency was promoted, the system of multilevel direct financing was accelerated, and the financial funds were used better to serve the real economy.

Vice Chairman ZHOU Mubing made a field trip to Fujian.

As of end-2014, 16 banks successfully launched 155 "Tools", with a total value of RMB 45.357 billion. Among the others, 110 "Tools" were still working and the total value was RMB 33.465 billion. There are other 10 banks making preparation for the launch of "Tools". All of these cover projects relating to the China (Shanghai) Pilot Free Trade Zone and Western Development and many industries, including agriculture, biopharmaceutical, hydraulics, high-tech industry, electricity, environmental protection industry, and so on. Besides, in order to provide more capital support to green economy, low-carbon economy, and circular economy through wealth management, banking institutions launched environment friendly direct financing tools for wealth management, focusing on green agriculture development, rural drinking water safety projects, energy-saving and environmental protection services and so on.

◎ Accelerating the establishment of a brand new E–ICBC

ICBC had adopted a proactive approach in adapting to new technological developments including big-data, cloud computing and mobile internet and in applying internet-based thinking to build a brand new E-ICBC. The Bank has established an internet financial service and operation system featured by the integration of five functions, namely payment, financing, financial transaction, commerce and information services as well as online-to-offline interaction. ICBC has built three platforms covering e-commerce, instant messaging and direct banking, and developed three product lines in e-payment, online financing as well as investment and wealth management. The Bank has also established a highly efficient and integrated online-to-offline service system.

◎ Zhongguanghe Finance company participated in the design of the first carbon bond

On May 12, 2014, Zhongguanghe Finance Company participated in the design of the first mid-term carbon bond product in China issued successfully in the interbank institutional investor market. As a brand new underlying asset, carbon bond was not only a significant innovative cross-sector bond product, that also a conducive exploration for promoting carbon derivatives in the future. By issuing the carbon bond the corporations were able to reduce the funding costs.

◎ Lanzhou Bank provided intelligent robot financial service

Taking the form of human body, the intelligent robot can provide service through human voices and body languages to welcome guests, draw tickets, introduce banking business, collecting phone fees and so on.

◎ Shanghai Pudong Development Bank realized integrated cell phone card, bank card and subway card payment business

In 2014, Shanghai Pudong Development Bank achieved cross-sector cooperation with Shentong Metro and China Mobile, integrating cell phone card, bank card and subway card into one for the first time. It released "China Mobile Pufa application for subway payment" integrating mobile payment, financial service and subway trip service together. Once business is activated, customers can swipe the cell phone directly to make subway payment in Shanghai and recharge and change subway card through cell phone application.

Box 6   Banks taking initiative to meet interest rate liberalization

First, in accordance with the overall requirements of comprehensively deepening reforms, the CBRC actively worked to accelerate the process of interest rate liberalization. In 2012, the CBRC set up the Interest Rate Liberalization Research Working Group. The Group studied the impact of interest rate liberalization on commercial banks and tried to work out coping strategy. Using the experience of other countries for reference, the CBRC organized quantitative calculation about the impact on banking industry caused by interest rate liberalization. It also joined the work of the State Council on interest rate liberalization.

Second, the CBRC specifically intensified the risk control on interest rate. The CBRC built the interest rate risk monitoring mechanism at some typical banking institutions and carried out regular monitoring on interest rate risk, through which the CBRC pushed the commercial banks to strengthen the risk control on interest rate. The CBRC also participated in the working group of Basel Committee on Banking Supervision on bank account interest rate risk.

Third, the CBRC urged commercial banks to improve their pricing capability and risk management capacity, so as to accelerate the business transformation. The CBRC urged them to improve their risk pricing mechanism, including optimizing pricing approaches, smoothing administrative process and promoting lean pricing management capacity. They made efforts to improve their ability to control interest rate risk, liquidity risk, and credit risk, and enhance the total risk management capacity. They were guided to build core competitiveness with their own characteristics with regard to strategic positioning, business model and financial innovation and thus become differentiators in the market.

III.Opening-up

In 2014, the CBRC set up the opening-up team which took the responsibility to coordinate the "bringing in" and "going global" of banking industry and encouraged Chinese banking institutions to support the overseas layout of Chinese-funded enterprises. At the same time, it promoted the opening-up in the banking industry which meant that with the prerequisite of effective supervision, it moderately erased the barrier for foreign banks entering into Chinese market, and with the pre-establishment national treatment and negative list, it expanded the market to Hong Kong and Macau banks, so as to encourage the benign competition in the banking industry.

1.Overseas development of Chinese banking institutions

By the end of 2014, 20 Chinese banking institutions set up over 1,200 outlets in 53 countries and jurisdictions with the total overseas assets reaching USD1.5 trillion.

In 2014, the China Development Bank officially set up its new Caracas Representative Office in Venezuela. The ICBC set up Mexico Subsidiary, London Branch and Rangoon Branch. The ABC set up Luxembourg Subsidiary, Russia Subsidiary and Sydney Subsidiary. The BOC set up Hungary Branch, Abu Dhabi Branch, Thailand Subsidiary and New Zealand Subsidiary. The CCB set up Toronto Branch, London Branch, Macau Branch and New Zealand Subsidiary. Moreover, the CCB acquired the Brazil BIC Bank. The BoCom set up Toronto Representative Office and Luxembourg Subsidiary. The China Minsheng Bank (CMBC) and Shanghai Pudong Development Bank (SPD) set up Singapore Branches. The China Merchants Bank (CMB) set up Luxembourg Branch, and its London Representative Office was upgraded to Branch. The China CITIC Bank set up London Representative Office. The Fudian Bank officially opened its joint venture bank in Laos.

In 2014, the Industrial Bank officially opened its Branch in Hong Kong. The Hua Xia Bank and Bohai Bank set up the Representative Offices in Hong Kong. The Bank of Dong Guan officially opened its Representative office in Hong Kong. The CMBC set up CMBC International Holdings Ltd. in Hong Kong. The Bank of Shanghai Hongkong, a fully subsidiary to Bank of Shanghai, set up Bank of Shanghai International in Hongkong The SPD Bank acquired Asiavest Partners Ltd. in Hong Kong. The Harbin Bank and Sheng Jing Bank went public on Hong Kong Stock Exchange.

2.The development of foreign banking institutions in China

By the end of 2014, banks from 15 countries and regions established 38 wholly foreign-owned banks (with 296 branches under them), 2 joint-venture banks (with 3 branches under them) and 1 wholly foreign-own finance company. 66 banks from 26 countries and regions established 97 branches in China. And 158 banks from 47 countries and regions established 182 Representative Office, 35 locally incorporated foreign banks, and 62 foreign bank branches were approved to conduct RMB business. 31 locally incorporated banks and 28 foreign bank branches were authorized to operate financial derivatives business. 6 locally incorporated foreign banks were approved to issue RMB financial bonds and 4 locally incorporated foreign banks were authorized to issue credit cards. 3 locally incorporated foreign banks were authorized to operate the businesses of securitization of credit assets.

Table 1   Foreign banking establishments in China (As of end-2014)

Unit: Number of banking institution

Institution/Type	Foreign banks	Wholly foreign-owned banks	Joint-venture banks	Wholly foreign-owned finance companies	Total
Locally incorporated institutions (LII)	—	38	2	1	41
LII branches and subsidiaries	—	296	3	—	299
Foreign bank branches	97	—	—	—	97
Sub-branches	16	537	10	—	563
Total	113	871	15	1	1,000

By the end of 2014, foreign banks maintained presence in 69 cities of 27 provinces, which largely formed a service network composed of head offices, branches and sub-branches with certain degree of market coverage and penetration. The total operating outlets amounted to 1,000, of which 17.2 percent located in northeast, middle and west of China. They played an active role in promoting finance coverage and balance the financial service. The total assets of foreign banking institutions increased to RMB 2,792.088 billion, with a year-on-year growth of 9.16 percent. The liabilities of these institutions totaled RMB 2,843.197 billion, with the year-on-year growth of 8.58 percent. The loans issued by these institutions totaled RMB 1,186.675 billion, up 7.22 percent year-on-year. In the meantime, their NPL ratio was 0.81 percent. Deposits totaled RMB 1,548,912 billion, up 3.74 percent year-on-year. Liquidity ratio registered 71.62 percent and after-tax profit recorded RMB 19,723 billion.

Table 2   Foreign banking assets in China (2010-2014)

Unit: RMB100 million, percent

Item/Year	2010	2011	2012	2013	2014
Asset	17,423	21,535	23,804	25,577[1]	27,921
As of the total banking assets in China	1.85	1.93	1.82	1.73	1.62

[1] This figure has been adjusted after the publishing date of the Annual Report.

By the end of 2014, a total of 14 Taiwan banks set up 2 locally incorporated banks (with 3 branches and 10 sub-branches), 18 branches directly affiliated to parent banks (with 7 sub-branches) and 3 representative offices in the mainland. And another 7 branches and 5 sub-branches were under preparation. The total operating outlets of Taiwan-owned banks amounted to over 50.

In 2014, the CBRC encouraged locally incorporated foreign banks to expand their financing channels. 4 locally incorporated foreign banks were authorized to operate the businesses of securitization of credit assets. And CBRC also supported locally incorporated foreign banks to operate businesses of securitization of credit assets in the interbank market.

Box 7   Opening-up of the mainland China's banking sector to foreign-owned banks

In November 2014, Premier Li Keqiang issued a Decree of the State Council and on December *20th the Decision of the State Council on the Amendments to Regulation on Administration of Foreign Banks* was announced. Against the background of comprehensively deepening reforms, this amendment is an active opening-up policy to foreign-owned banks. The key points of amendments are based on the real conditions of foreign-owned banks operation in China. With the prerequisite of effective supervision, China would moderately erase some requirements of entering into and operating RMB businesses to the foreign-owned banks and provide easier and more independent institutional environment to the establishment of foreign-owned banks in China.

(1) Implement three actions to further open the mainland market to foreign-owned banks. In accordance with the amended *Regulations on Administration of Foreign Banks*, since January 1st, 2015 three actions would be implemented: first, remove the stipulation of minimum operating capital of branches of locally incorporated foreign banks in mainland China; second, cancel the stipulation that the representative office must be established before setting up foreign-owned banking institutions; third,

the minimum operation time is reduced from 3 years to 1 year for the foreign banks before they apply for RMB businesses and the requirement of making profit in two consecutive years is also removed accordingly.

(2) Based on the principle of mutual benefit, the CBRC promoted the opening-up in the banking sector. The CBRC carried out and implemented the Belt and Road initiative, and took part in bilateral and multilateral negotiations (including the agreement of investment between mainland and Hong Kong Macau, China-America, China-Europe, China-Korea, China-Australia, and China-Brazil and FTA negotiations), so that, the CBRC could raise the level of opening-up in the banking sector.

(3) Simplifying items of administrative examination and approval and facilitating the process to get authorization. In September, the CBRC issued the *Regulations of CBRC on Items of Administrative Examination for Foreign Banks*, in which 11 items of administrative examination for foreign banks were removed. In the meantime, it further specified the importance of intensifying supervision during and after relevant business and unifying the principle in regulation.

Box 8   Further opening-up of the mainland China's banking sector to Hong Kong and Macau

In December 2014, the *Agreement on Primarily Free Trade and Services between Guangdong and Hong Kong/Macau under CEPA* (Closer

Economic Partnership Arrangement) was signed and it would officially come into force on March 1st, 2015. Under the framework of CEPA, the CBRC put forward the first Negative List of banking on opening-up and further opened the mainland China to Hong Kong and Macau banks with the Pre-Establishment National Treatment and Negative List, so that in Guangdong province, the CBRC mostly liberalized the trade in services of banking between mainland and Hong Kong and Macau. Except for the businesses on the Negative List, Hong Kong and Macau banks enjoyed the same treatment in Guangdong as mainland banks. This policy demonstrated the promise from mainland that the market was opened to Hong Kong and Macau banks, which further extended the space of development of Hong Kong and Macau banks in the mainland.

◎ The CBRC Guangdong Office vigorously promoted the deepening financial cooperation between Guangdong and Hong Kong, Macao and Taiwan

Considering the regional features of Guangdong, the CBRC Guangdong Office actively implemented the pertinent provisions in CEPA 9 with the lowering of eligibility requirements in total assets to USD4 billion for Macao's banking institutions to set up in Hengqin, together with the provision to allow the eligible financial institutions of Hong Kong and Macao to establish consumer finance companies in Guangdong. In 2014, the Luso International Banking Limited opened a representative office in Henqin, marking the historical breakthrough of the first Macao's banking institution to set up in Guangdong province. In the meantime, the preferential policy for Hong Kong's banking institutions has been furthered implemented, as the cross-city sub-branches of Hong Kong's banking institutions had spread all over the prefecture-level cities in Guangdong. While Taiwan's banking institutions had already set up two branches in Guangdong, two more were in the process of establishment, and some of the established branches had been approved to engage in RMB business for Taiwan companies.

Box 9   Further deepening the cross-strait banking cooperation

On December 25th, 2014, the forth cross-stait banking regulation consultation was held in Beijing. Shang Fulin, the chairman of CBRC, and the principal of banking regulation institution from Taiwan had a meeting, and both side communicated over the proposal of strengthening cooperation between banking regulation institutions from two sides. Mainland and Taiwan would build a joint research mechanism of reform on banking regulation. In order to maintain the cross-strait financial stability and avoid financial risks, two sides agreed that primarily based on the *MOU of Management Cooperation on Cross-strait Banking Regulation*, cooperation on crisis management would be futher enhanced to maintain cross-strait financial stability and prevent risks.

Thanks to the cross-strait regulation cooperation mechanism, the financial cooperation between Taiwan and Mainland made great progress. By the end of 2014, a total of 14 Taiwan banks set up 2 locally incorporated banks (with 3 branches and 10 sub-branches), 18 branches directly affiliated to parent banks (with 7 sub-branches) and 3 representative offices in the mainland. Another 7 branches and 5 sub-branches were under preparation. The total operating outlets of Taiwan-owned banks would amount to over 50. Mainland banks set up 3 branches and 1 representative office in Taiwan. Meanwhile, the CBRC actively support branches of Taiwan banks in mainland to operate RMB businesses and increase operating capital. By the end of 2014, 1 subsidiary and 10 branches of Taiwan banks were approved to conduct RMB business, besides that, in 2014, the CBRC approved Taiwan banks to raise new capital amounting to RMB 1.9 billion.

◎ The CBRC Xiamen Office promoted cross–strait banking cooperation

The CBRC Xiamen Office proactively supported the development of cross-strait RMB correspondent bank for settlement and clearing. By the year end of 2014, 38 RMB settlement accounts had been opened by Taiwan banks with their Xiamen counterparts, with the settlement volume amounting to 2/3 of the Fujian Province. The over-the-counter currency exchange in Xiamen recorded as TWD 580m, up 7.8 percent YoY. Bank of China launched cross-strait RMB cash distribution and collection service through Xiamen branch. In 2014, the branch dealt 25 batches of RMB distribution and 37 batches collection, with the value of RMB272 million and RMB2.628 billion respectively, providing a new service option to Taiwan banks. Agriculture Bank of China, Bank of Communications and Bank of Xiamen had set up stand-alone service centers to facilitate the service to Taiwan enterprises and business.

Part Three

Supporting Economic Restructuring, Transformation and Upgrading

- Tapping the idle capital while making good use of incremental capital
- Financial support to key areas and industries
- Financial inclusion
- Addressing overcapacity and promoting green credit
- Fully promoting balanced regional development

I. Tapping the idle capital while making good use of incremental capital

1. Optimizing credit policies and expanding financing channels. First, banking institutions were urged to further improve differentiated credit policies and adopt a variety of means to address excessive and backward capacities. Second, efforts were made to revise policies concerning the disposal and write-off of non-performing assets (NPAs). As a result, more channels were created for the disposal of banking NPAs, and more autonomy was given to banks in the disposal of non-performing loans (NPLs). Third, policies regarding credit asset securitization were further improved, shifting from the examination and approval system to the registration and filing system. Fourth, listed banks were encouraged to issue preferred shares on a pilot basis, thus providing a new financing instrument for capital replenishment. Fifth, private investors were encouraged to invest in the banking industry with supporting supervisory rules improved accordingly.

2. Optimizing capital allocation and improving financial services. First, banking institutions were guided to adjust their credit extension plans and meet the credit needs of advanced manufacturing and strategic emerging industries, modern IT industry and information consumption, renovation and upgrading of conventional industries, service industry, and green and environmental protection industries. Second, financial services were optimized for MSEs, particularly micro and small high-tech, innovative companies and start-ups, with financial resources consolidated to support their development. Third, banking institutions were encouraged to strengthen agro-related financial services and credit support for farmers, agriculture modernization, new-type agricultural businesses, and agricultural products wholesale sector. Fourth, banking institutions were supported to actively meet rural and urban households' reasonable needs for consumer loans, thus facilitating the upgrading of domestic consumption. Fifth, efforts were made to actively support the reasonable credit needs of projects under construction and qualified for renewed construction, major infrastructure building, urban infrastructure building as well as people's livelihood programs such as low-income housing.

Box 10   The pilot project of credit asset securitization made positive progress

In 2014, the CBRC actively promoted the normalization of credit asset securitization. First, it issued the **Notice on Registration and Filing Process for Credit Asset Securitization**, marking the transition from the examination and approval system to the registration and filing system for the issuance of securitized products. Secondly, it issued the **Public Announcement** ([2013] No. 21) jointly with the PBC, which contains revised regulations on risk retention, allowing the originating institutions to adopt a more flexible approach to risk retention and thereby release capital more effectively. Thirdly, it encouraged the inclusion of credit assets into the asset pool provided that such assets conform to national industrial policies with equal consideration of benefits and orientation. Efforts were also made to study new-type underlying assets that serve the real economy, such as MSE loans and personal consumer loans. Fourth, efforts were made to explore credit asset securitization in the stock market, expand the scope of institutional investors eligible for securitized products, and prevent risk transmission within the banking industry. In 2014, 47 institutions issued credit asset-backed securities (ABSs) worth RMB282 billion in the inter-bank and exchange markets. The originators of credit asset securitization were expanded and the underlying assets further diversified. In 2014, 7 trust companies were granted trustee license for special purpose trusts, and the number of asset securitization trustees was on the rise.

Thematic column 2 Improving credit availability and affordability for enterprises

In 2014, China's economy shifted to the phase of new normal, with the gear changing from high speed to a medium-to-high speed growth. The economy was restructured in that its focus changed from quantity and capacity building to quality and capacity adjustment. The increasing operational pressures and rising lending risk premium faced by companies gradually took effect on their financing cost and borrowing needs. In response, the CBRC adopted a range of policy measures to address MSEs' difficulties in accessing and affording funding resources.

(1) Efforts were made to curb unreasonable funding cost rise in the banking industry, enhance the diversification and stability of funding sources, and make good use of idle capital. In September, the CBRC issued, jointly with the MOF and the PBC, the *Notice on Strengthening Deposit Deviation Management of Commercial Banks* ([2014] No. 236), stipulating that the month-end deposit deviation ratio of commercial banks shall not exceed 3%, thus urging commercial banks to strengthen the management of deposit stability and appropriately control their month-end deposit deviation ratio. The CBRC continued to expand the pilot of credit asset securitization. More institutions, including city commercial banks, rural commercial banks, foreign banks and financial leasing companies were included into the scope of originators. The underlying asset types were also expanded. The examination and approval process was improved in terms of efficiency. In addition, efforts were made to promote the credit asset transfer business operated by the Credit Asset Registration & Exchange. In 2014, 47 institutions issued credit ABS worth RMB282 billion in the inter-bank and stock markets. Commercial banks issued more MSE financial bonds and agro-related

financial bonds. The examination and approval efficiency was improved. The CBRC continued to support eligible commercial banks to issued MSE financial bonds, with the size of MSE financial bonds continuing to grow. As of end-2014, the CBRC had approved the issuance of MSE financial bonds worth RMB419 billion and agro-related financial bonds worth 26.5 billion. The CBRC also adjusted the calculation methods of loan-to-deposit ratio. In June, it issued the *Notice on Adjusting Loan-to-Deposit Calculation Methods for Commercial Banks*, according to which agro-related and MES loans are deducted from the numerator (loans) with a view to releasing capital in support of MSEs.

(2) Efforts were made to shorten the financing chains of companies, advance their restructuring in inter-bank and wealth management businesses, and eliminate unnecessary funding "channels". In April, the CBRC issued, jointly with the PBOC, CSRC, CIRC and SAFE, the *Notice on Regulating Inter-bank Businesses of Financial Institutions* (Yin Fa [2014] No. 127), aiming to regulate inter-bank businesses and strengthen the internal and external management of such businesses. In May, it issued the *Notice on Standardizing the Management of Inter-bank Businesses of Commercial Banks;* in October, it issued the *Notice on Carrying out Thematic Inspection over the Implementation of New Rules on Interbank Business by Banking Institutions*. Afterwards, it rolled out on-site examinations over the rules and processes, business operation, accounting practices, capital and provisioning calculation of banking institutions. In July, it issued the *Notice on Issues Related to Improving the Organization and Management System of Wealth Management Business of Banks*, pushing banking institutions to undertake

wealth management business unit reform based on the principles of "separate accounting, risk segregation, conduct regulation and centralized management". The CBRC continued to advance two innovative pilot projects, namely "Direct Financing Instrument for Wealth Management" and "Banking Wealth Management Plan". More banks were involved in these pilot projects. The planned goals of "eliminating unnecessary channels, shortening financing chains and de-leveraging" were achieved, effectively facilitating the direct match between lenders and borrowers.

(3) The CBRC carried out thematic inspections over banking fee businesses and cleaned up the unfair charges against supervisory rules. In February, the CBRC and NDRC issued the *Rules on Service Charges of Commercial Banks* (CBRC and NDRC Decree No. 1, 2014). In June, thematic inspection over banking charges was rolled out, focusing on institutional building, internal management, price transparency, fee charging practice, compliant handling mechanism and accountability system of banking institutions. In the meantime, it organized training sessions on policies of banking service charges to facilitate market players to strengthen pricing management.

(4) Loan approval and extension became more efficient, and unnecessary "bridges" were removed. In March, the CBRC issued the *Guiding Opinions on MSE Financial Services in 2014*, emphasizing that the CBRC would adhere to differentiated supervision and continue to guide banks to improve financial services for MSEs. In July, it issued the *Notice on Improving and Innovating MSE Loan Services and Upgrading MSE Financial Services*, aiming to address the issue of high-interest "bridge" financing faced by MSEs and encourage banking institutions to reduce MSE financing cost by means of loan renewal, annual-review-based lending and revolving loans, etc..

(5) Commercial banks were guided to improve the appraisal and evaluation management system and shift away from profit-and-size-driven operating philosophy. In June, the CBRC issued the *Notice on Conducting Special Evaluation of Commercial Banks' Performance Appraisal*, urging banking institutions to correct the profit-driven and asset-size-driven operating philosophy, optimize internal appraisal mechanisms and establish a sound performance review system. The *Notice* also required banking institutions to carry out self-assessment and CBRC departments and local offices to conduct supervisory evaluations and random inspections in accordance with applicable regulations.

(6) The CBRC improved policies governing financing guarantee to regulate the pricing practices. In July, it issued the *Guiding Opinions on Promoting Financing Guarantee Institutions to Serve MSEs and Agro-related Development*, which clearly stipulates that financing guarantee institutions must set fees and charges at a reasonable level and may not impose unreasonable requirements or involve in illegal possession of funds. Furthermore, the CBRC made field trips to monitor MSE loan guarantees and regulate the pricing practices of financing guarantee institutions. As a result, the practice of transferring hidden burdens to MSEs by some guarantee institutions was curbed. Efforts were made to accelerate the government-led development of re-guarantee institutions. The CBRC also coordinated local finance authorities and other agencies to give more policy support to financing guarantee institutions, thus expanding credit enhancement effect of MSE financing. In July, the CBRC issued the *Guiding Opinions on Improving Financial Support to Scale Agricultural Production and Intensive Management* [Yin Jian Fa [2014] No. 38] jointly with the Ministry of Agriculture, guiding banking institutions to work with agro-related financing guarantee institutions to explore the use of rural financing guarantee fund to improve farmers' credit rating and provide better protection against credit risks.

In December 2014, the average weighted loan rate for non-financial corporations and other sectors was 6.77 percent, down by 0.42 percentage point from the year beginning. Among others, the average weighted interest rate for general loans and bill financing was 6.92 percent and 5.67 percent respectively, down by 0.22 percentage point and 1.87 percentage points respectively from year beginning. At the end of 2014, the yield to maturity of 3-year and 7-year AA corporate bond in the interbank market stood at 5.85 percent and 6.34 percent respectively, down by 1.50 and 12.7 percentage points respectively.

◎ China's first issue of agro-related financial bonds

In 2014, the CBRC granted approvals to Leshan Commercial Bank, Suzhou Bank, Harbin Bank, Laishang Bank and Huishang Bank to issue financial bonds for agro-related development in the interbank bond market with a total value of RMB24.5 billion.

Among others, Suzhou Bank took the lead to issue RMB2 billion worth of such financial bonds on September 30, 2014.

The bond issuance helped to expand new funding sources for banks in a bid to support agro-related development and encourage stable inflow of long-term funds to rural areas. It will also encourage commercial banks to explore active liabilities and improve their management.

◎ The CBRC Henan Office optimize the funding environment for Micro and Small Enterprises (MSEs)

The CBRC Henan Office actively promoted the implementation of loan risk compensation mechanism for MSEs in Henan province. 11 out of 18 cities in Henan established the MSE loan risk compensation or assistance fund. In 2014, the compensation funds totaled more than RMB1 billion at both provincial and city level. Together with the Department of Industry and Information Technology in Henan, the CBRC Henan Office organized the loan matching activities for the banking institutions and MSEs. The activities attracted a total of 13,088 enterprises to participate, with 10,317 enterprises successfully signing the contracts and total loans valuing at RMB94.69 billion. At the end of 2014, the balance of MSE loans in Henan rose by RMB159.997 or 25.99 percent to RMB775.57 billion from year beginning.

II. Financial support to key areas and industries

1.Supporting national strategies and the development of experimental economic zones

Efforts were made to improve financial support to the implementation of national strategies, such as the Belt and Road Initiative, and the coordinated development of the Beijing-Tianjin-Hebei area as well as China (Shanghai) Pilot Free Trade Zone (SFTZ). In 2014, the CBRC actively studied how to improve financial support for the Belt and Road Initiative, strengthened the communication and coordination with national or local financial regulators of the countries along the Belt and Road area, and proactively facilitated the endeavors to signing MOUs on bilateral banking supervisory cooperation with countries yet to establish supervisory cooperation mechanisms with China. It encouraged banking institutions to strengthen financial cooperation with the countries or regions along the Belt and Road and devise appropriate means and measures in business expansion and branch establishment, to support the Initiative. The China Development Bank has largely built the repository of major projects along the Belt and Road and set out preferential credit policies. The Export-Import Bank of China has also made active efforts to promote infrastructure projects of host countries and support the development of interconnectivity projects. Commercial banks have also accelerated the establishment of offices and business development in the countries and regions along the Belt and Road.

Thematic column 3　The development of banking industry in China (Shanghai) Pilot Free Trade Zone (SFTZ)

On May 12, 2014, the CBRC authorized its Shanghai Office to issue the *Notice on the Institutional Arrangements of Banking Supervision in the China (Shanghai) Pilot Free Trade Zone*, based on the *Notice on Issues concerning Banking Supervision in China (Shanghai) Pilot Free Trade Zone* and the *Opinions on the Licensing of Offshore Banking Activities in China (Shanghai) Pilot Free Trade Zone*. The basic framework for supervising the banking industry in the free trade zone has preliminarily taken shape. In June 2014, the CBRC Shanghai Office set up the SFTZ Banking Supervision Department dedicated to promoting the oversight and innovation of banking activities and improving the supervisory efficiency within the zone.

The supervisory regime for the banking industry in the pilot zone has 6 distinct features. Firstly, the administration is streamlined, powers delegated, and licensing procedures simplified. For banking sun-branches (including offices below the sub-branch level) in the SFTZ, an ex-post reporting requirement, instead of the existing pre-approval, will be applied for items regarding the application for establishing such entities and qualifications for corresponding executives. Secondly, in-process and ex-post supervision is strengthened. A relatively independent banking supervisory reporting system was established to strengthen continuous monitoring and analysis of innovations and risk profiles of banking institutions in the pilot zone. In particular, it emphasizes post assessment of the supervisory work. Thirdly, an inclusive approach that covers all risks is stressed, highlighting the special risk management requirements in the SFTZ. Fourthly, the supervisory approaches are optimized and emphasis is laid on self-discipline of institutions and practitioners. Fifthly, the regulatory requirements applicable to both domestic and foreign banking institutions are harmonized so as to boost the openness and competition. Sixthly, banking institutions in the SFTZ are allowed to explore

business operations within and outside the SFTZ as well as in overseas markets.

As of end-2014, 54 operating outlets of 49 banking institutions were granted with approvals to operate in the SFTZ, including 1 incorporated bank, 16 branches and 5 sub-branches of Chinese banks, 25 sub-branches of foreign banks, 2 branches of financial asset management companies, 2 financial leasing companies and 3 finance companies. ICBC and BOC has built head-office-level cross-border financial service platform based on their branches in the SFTZ, thus further optimizing bank-wide management framework for cross-border businesses. The China Merchants Bank (CMB) has established the Free Trade Finance Management Department in its Shanghai Branch to manage and guide the development of its banking businesses in the SFTZ. The SFZT Branch of Ping An Bank assumes the responsibilities of studying, promoting and managing bank-wide free-trade-related businesses.

Pursuant to the *Reply of the State Council on Approving the Expansion of China (Shanghai) Pilot Free Trade Zone* (Guo Han [2014] No. 179), the SFTZ was officially extended to cover Lujiazui Financial Area, Jinqiao Development Zone Area and Zhangjiang Hi-tech Area. As of end-2014, there were 94 banking offices in the SFTZ. The deposits and loans of these offices accounted for 64% and 67% respectively of the city-wide total. In addition, there were 21 non-bank financial institutions that fell into 7 categories, accounting for 46% of the total number of non-bank financial institutions in Shanghai. Their deposits and loans accounted for 42% and 60% respectively of the city-wide total.

The banking industry in the SFTZ has four features. Firstly, trade financing activities were robust. The trade financing of banking clients in the SFTZ accounted for about 19.81% of all loans. Secondly, offshore businesses were growing fast. The offshore loans and deposits of the branches of 4 Chinese commercial banks in the SFTZ added up to USD1.5

billion and 5.6 billion respectively. All their offshore asset businesses were classified as "Normal". Thirdly, demands for cross-border financing and global funds management were thriving. In 2014, the overseas RMB-denominated borrowings of companies in the SFTZ stood at over RMB30 billion. The two-way cross-border RMB cash pooling transactions of banking clients in the SFTZ reached nearly RMB200 billion. Fourthly, the free trade accounting unit (FTU) businesses under free trade accounts (FTAs) were increasing . Ten Chinese commercial banks have cumulatively opened around 10,000 FTAs, with total assets amounting to around RMB30.3 billion. The financing cost is about 10% lower than that out of SFTZ. Low-cost overseas funds were effectively leveraged.

◎ The CBRC Shenzhen Office help boost the development of Qianhai Area

The CBRC Shenzhen Office actively explored the pilot programs of establishing private banks and the corresponding regulatory mode, under which it guided the WeBank to become the first batch of piloting private banks and the first to open business. It also guided the efforts of Wing Lung Bank and China Unicom in jointly establishing a consumer finance company, namely Merchants Union Consumer Finance Company Limited, which became the first consumer finance company to be established in Guangdong Province under CEPA framework. It supported one of the Taiwan banks to establish headquarters in Qianhai area, and actively promoted the Shenzhen Rural Commercial Bank to initiate the establishment of a financial leasing company in Qianhai area. At present, 28 banking institutions have set up outlets in Qianhai, with the industrial cluster effects gradually taking shape. Meanwhile, the CBRC Shenzhen Office promoted the financial institutions to explore innovative business in the aspects of cross-boarder operations, off-shore financial actives and Qianhai factors platform construction so as to support the development and opening-up of Qianhai area.

◎ Huaxia Bank launched the China's First Beijing-Tianjin-Hebei integration debit card

In response to Beijing-Tianjin-Hebei Coordinated Development Program, a national strategic development program that Beijing and neighboring Tianjin and Hebei province coordinate their development for the purpose of regional integration, Huaxia Bank launched Beijing-Tianjin-Hebei Integration Debit Card on October 9, 2014, with the aim to fostering the collaboration of business, products, service and development. By launching this debit card, Huaxia Bank could provide integrated services in different outlets, expense deduction, wealth management, VIP service, loans and finance, Corporate Card and payment facilities. Card holders could enjoy the same and synchronized services in Beijing, Tianjin and Hebei, and obtain loans in one city backed up by mortgages and pledges registered in the other two. By the end of 2014, Huaxia Bank had issued a total of more than 40,000 Beijing-Tianjin-Hebei Integration Debit Cards in Beijing.

2. Supporting strategic emerging industries

The CBRC encouraged banks to strengthen credit support for key development areas of strategic emerging industries, and provide preferential policies in credit facilities, interest rate pricing and means of pledge. Banks were required to communicate and collaborate with governments at all levels to establish a mechanism to coordinate between credit policy and national policies in support of strategic emerging industries. As of end-2014, the outstanding loans to strategic emerging industries extended by 21 major banks (including policy banks, large commercial banks, joint-stock commercial banks and Postal Savings Bank of China) reached RMB2, 212.58 billion, an increase of RMB66.76 billion compared with year beginning. Loans were relatively concentrated in the areas of energy conservation, environmental protection, new energy, new materials and new generation information technology, with the outstanding balance of RMB889.06 billion, RMB664.73 billion, RMB237.13 billion and RMB194.16 billion respectively, accounting for 40.2 percent, 30.0 percent, 10.7 percent and 8.8 percent respectively out of the total loan balance of strategic emerging industries.

Chart 8   Breakdown of loans to strategic emerging industries by 21 major banks as of end-2014

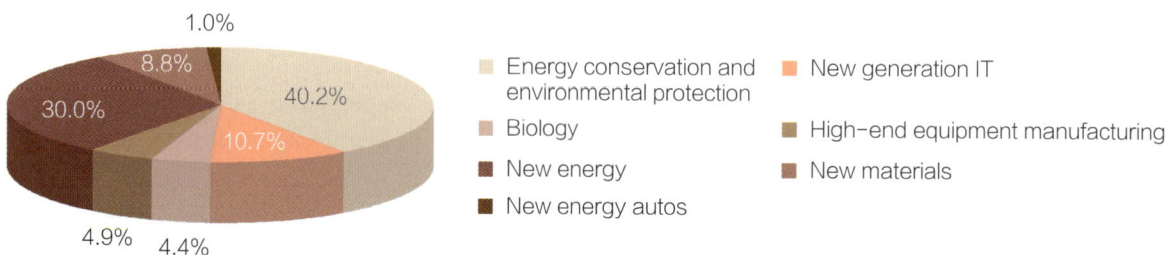

■ Energy conservation and environmental protection	■ New generation IT
■ Biology	■ High-end equipment manufacturing
■ New energy	■ New materials
■ New energy autos	

3.Supporting the development of the culture industry

By jointly issuing the *Opinions on Effectively Promoting Institutional Innovation and Providing Financial Services for Sci-Tech Development* (Yin Fa [2014] No. 9) with PB, MIT, CSRC, CIRC, and SIPO, the CBRC guided banking institutions to support the innovations of the culture industry by promoting the use of intellectual properties as a pledge. A comprehensive survey was conducted to review the use of warehouse receipts, insurance policies, equities and intellectual properties as pledges, thus facilitating the preparations for the development of policy measures regarding relevant pledged loans. By the end of 2014, a total of RMB532.81 billion loans were extended to the culture industry by 21 major banks, up 12.3% from the year beginning. Loans were relatively concentrated in the areas of tourist spots management, arts and crafts making, other culture & art sectors, and cable radio & television transmission services, with the outstanding balance standing at RMB113.54 billion, RMB64.05 billion, RMB55.19 billion and RMB34.16 billion respectively, and accounting for 21.3 percent, 12.0 percent, 10.4 percent and 6.4 percent respectively of the total loans issued to the culture industry.

Chart 9   Breakdown of loans to key areas in the culture industry by 21 major banks as of end-2014

■ Management of tourist spots	■ Other culture & art sectors
■ Arts and crafts making	■ Cable radio & television transmission Services
■ Cultural relics & intangible cultural heritage protection	■ Television
■ Art performance venues	■ Others

◎ The Export-Import Bank of China behind the "Go Global" endeavour of China's culture industry

By the end of 2014, the Export-Import Bank of China had lent to over 60% overseas cultural projects that applied for loans across the country. It is now the largest financial institution in China, both by project quantity and by outstanding loan volume, in supporting China's culture going global initiatives. Key projects that the Bank has supported include the acquisition of the White House Theatre in Branson, USA, by Heaven Creation Entertainment; the International Entertainment Show of Yunnan Cultural Investment Group; the overseas investment by Startimes Telecommunication and Internet Technology Corporation; and the acquisition of AMC theatres by Dalian Wanda Group. Such cultural going global projects have assisted Chinese culture companies to expand their share in the international market, and to improve their management scheme, therefore extending the reach and influence of the Chinese culture industry.

◎ Bank of China explored innovative financial products and services to support culture industry development

In response to the funding difficulties faced by culture industry, such as large scale of intangible assets and lack of mortgages and guarantees, Bank of China developed a batch of credit products tailored to culture industry, which were backed up by pledges of future beneficiary rights, insurance and entrustments. In this way it provided funding support to the cultural development of intangible cultural heritage, such as celadon porcelain, stone carving, Suzhou embroidery and black wood carving.

4. Supporting low-income housing projects

Banking institutions were guided to strengthen credit support for low-income housing projects under the principle of risks controllable and business viable and with innovative financing models. On July 25, 2014, the CBRC approved China Development Bank (CDB) to open the Housing Finance Business Unit. The approved business scope is to extend loans for the renovation of shanty areas included in the national renovation program for shanty areas and relevant urban infrastructure projects. As of end-2014, the outstanding balance of bank loans to low-income housing projects was RMB1, 250 billion, up 53.7% year on year. Among such loans, RMB843.7 billion was extended to the renovation of shanty houses and dilapidated buildings in reclamation areas, accounting for 67.5 percent of the total loans to low-income housing projects.

◎ Exploring the "Beijing approach" to support the renovation of shanty areas

Under the guidance of the CBRC Beijing Office, the China Development Bank Beijing Branch explored the "Beijing approach" to support the renovation of shanty areas, which was a unified credit platform building upon the Beijing Public Housing Center. This platform came out with a special model of "Pre-Authorization for Credit & Approval", which approves mature projects on a batch-by-batch basis. By the end of 2014, CDB Beijing Branch extended a total of RMB49.06 billion loans to the renovation of shanty areas. Thus it was named the outstanding player in supporting Beijing public housing endeavor for the past 5 years.

◎ The CBRC Inner Mongolia Office accelerated the financial service to low-income housing

The CBRC Inner Mongolia Office promoted the renovation of shanty areas in Beiliang District of Baotou, Dongsheng District of Erodes and Shengong District of Hulunbeier through repurchasing vacant houses, transforming housing belt and resettling dislocated individuals in a centralized manner. The experiences of Beiliang District were reported by CCTV and other famous media.

Old view of shanty town in Beiliang, Baoto.

Morning group exercise in the newly built community of Beiliang, Baoto.

Box 11   Supporting the creation of the National Integrated Circuit(IC) Industry Fund

In 2014, the State Council issued the *Notice of the State Council on Issuing the Outline of Promoting the Development of Integrated Circuit Industry* (Guo Fa [2014] No. 4) and the *Outline of Promoting the Development of Integrated Circuit Industry*.

The CBRC participated in the coordination meeting of the National IC Industry Development Steering Group to make policy recommendations for providing financial support to the IC industry. It supported China Development Bank Capital Corporation, a wholly-owned subsidiary of CDB, to participate in the creation of the National IC Industry Fund. In the mean time, it encouraged and guided CDB, China Exim Bank and other banks to strengthen credit support for the IC industry with innovative financing models.

III. Financial inclusion

On November 12, 2013, The Third Plenary Session of the 18th Communist Party of China Central Committee officially included promotion of financial inclusion as an important part of the comprehensive deepened reform endeavors. According to the requirements of the taskforce on Taskforce of the State Council on Tackling International Financial Crisis, the CBRC led the efforts in setting up the State Council Financial Inclusion Research Team, consisting of members from 14 ministries and commissions, including the PBC and MOF. The Research Team has completed 5 research projects, including the *International Experience in Financial Inclusion,* and submitted the *Research Report: Developing Financial Inclusion in China* to the State Council. The Report outlines feasible strategies for financial inclusion in China. Financial inclusion must be built on the basis of equal opportunities and business sustainability. Efforts should be made to increase policy support, strengthen the financial system and improve financial infrastructure, so as to provide suitable and effective financial services at affordable costs to all organizations and individuals in need of financial services.

1. Financial Services for Micro and Small Enterprises (MSEs)

(1) Strengthening regulatory guidance

In March, the CBRC issued the *Guiding Opinions on Financial Services to Micro and Small Enterprises*, requiring banks to upgrade financial services to MSEs. Banks were guided to achieve steady credit growth, improve the outlay of institutional outlets, strengthen positive incentives, and promote the development of the information service system and the credit enhancement system with a view to addressing the lack of information and the shortage of credit faced by MSEs. Between April 27 and 29, the CBRC led the efforts to oversee the implementation of the *Opinions of the State Council on Further Supporting the Healthy Development of MSEs* (Guo Fa [2012] No. 14) and related policies. On June 30, the CBRC issued the *Notice on Adjusting Loan-to-Deposit Calculation Methods for Commercial Banks*, according to which the loan calculation no longer counts in MSE loans, so as to guide banks to extend more loans to MSEs.

(2) Promoting experience sharing and ensuring the ultimate policy implementation

On May 15, 2014, the CBRC launched the Third MSE Financial Service Month campaign with the theme of "Supporting MSEs, Promoting Upgrading, Preventing Risks and Benefiting People". The CBRC guided its local offices to organize a variety of publicity activities, such as publicity shows, bank-enterprise connection, thematic forums, etc.. A special column themed "Upgrading Financial Services to MSEs" was created in the *Financial Digest*, featuring articles about banks' experiences in serving MSEs. On November 17, the CBRC held a video conference on MSE financial services, requiring banking institutions to increase credit support to MSEs and adopt differentiated supervisory policies regarding the issue of special purpose financial bonds; they were also required to continuously promote financial innovation, improve their business procedures and processes and information systems with Big Data and other technologies, expand service offerings and extend service duration; in addition, they were required to defend the bottom line of risks, judge the risks of MSEs from the long-term perspective, and improve the means of risk resolution; they were also instructed to eliminate unfair fees and charges and shorten the financing chain, thus effectively reducing the funding cost for MSEs.

As of end-2014, the balance of MSE loans was RMB20.7 trillion, accounting for 23.9% of the total loan balance, up by RMB3.08 trillion from year beginning, and by RMB173.1 billion or 17.5% year on year. The growth rate was 4.2 percentage points higher than the total loan growth average, achieving the set growth targets for the past five consecutive years. 114.46 million MSEs were granted loans, up by 9.0 percent year on year. Around 3,000 banking outlets, 4,000 specialized sub-branches and over 1,100 new-type rural financial institutions provided financial services to MSEs.

Box 12   Banking institutions supported the development of E-commerce in rural areas

In recent years, driven by the platform of E-commerce, a number of "E-commerce villages" comprising of micro and small online shops came into being, such as Qingyanliu Village in Zhejiang's Yiwu and Dongfeng Village in Jiangsu's Suining. In 2014, the CBRC conducted a survey on 20 E-commerce villages in 7 provinces. The survey showed that banking institutions took a range of measures to support micro and small online shops in rural areas, including: extending credit line on a village-by-village basis, promoting the financial inclusion, leveraging online credit resources, offering flexible credit products, and reducing e-stores' burden by offering discounts. Recognizing that industrial organizations are becoming intelligent, specialized and small in size under the economic new normal, banking institutions made active efforts to adapt and provide support to new forms of business operations, such as micro and small online stores in rural areas. Considering that emerging start-ups and MSEs are dependent on information and the Internet, they made service improvements and product innovations, and focused more on supporting the combination of new generation IT and conventional industries, expansion of domestic demands and upgrading of consumption, and promotion of financial inclusion in rural areas. They actively identified and developed new growth areas, provided new dynamics for the real economy, and pursued the transformation and upgrading of their own and the industry as a whole.

◎ The CBRC Chongqing Office promoted innovation of credit maturity, repayment, mortgages and pledges of credit products to MSEs

The CBRC Chongqing Office drafted the *Guiding Opinions on Improving Financial Services to Ease Funding Difficulties and Reduce Funding Cost* and implemented three mechanisms (i.e. the daily monitoring and inspecting mechanism, evaluation and assessment mechanism and regulatory accountability system), and urged banks to speed up the innovation in credit duration, ways of repayment, special business unit (SBU) and bank-corporate connection. It also implemented"Two Bans and One Exemption" to reduce the external hidden burden of financing for enterprises. Banking institutions in Chongqing piloted a credit product with revolving credit line that could be effective for 10 years at most, while some banks have also realized on-line self-service application of such products. By the end of 2014，the balance of loans with innovative repayment was RMB51.94 billion, accounting for 11.4 percent of the total MSE loans, up by 54.6 percent from year beginning; the balance of loans with innovative maturities was RMB337.18 billion, up by 22.5 percent from year beginning.

◎ The CBRC Xinjiang Office innovated SME financial services with ethnical features

To strengthen financial service innovation, the CBRC Xinjiang Office promoted local banking institutions to promote SME financial innovation with 55 innovative products developed. Through the innovated cooperation mode of "ethnical industrial fund plus ethnic affairs commission plus ethnical businesses plus banks plus government", the banking institutions in Xinjiang have stepped up the financial support to MSEs with 200 loans issued and a total balance of RMB2.545 billion, thus further promoted the development of industries with ethnic features.

2. Financial services in rural areas

In 2014, the CBRC drafted the *Report on Implementing the Financial Inclusion Requirement and Promoting the Development of Rural Financial Service System,* setting forth the overall goals and specific actions for promoting the development of rural financial service system. The Report aimed to promote the level of financial inclusion and specified a number of actions to deepen financial reform in rural areas,

Vice Chairman GUO Ligen made a field trip to Sichuan to guide banking institutions to support the development of modern agriculture.

diversified financial service providers, and actively built a sustainable, multi-layered inclusive financial service system in the rural areas.

(1) Optimizing differentiated supervisory approaches. The CBRC set up a "green" licensing channel for financial institutions that offered innovative agro-related products and/or established outlets in under-banked areas. The methods for calculating loan-to-deposit ratio were adjusted. The items of agro-related re-lending and agro-related financial bonds were exempted from being computed as the numerator (or loans) of loan-to-deposit calculation. Banks incorporated at the county level were required to set aside a certain proportion of loans for local borrowers. Banking institutions were guided to increase the weight of agro-related businesses when appraising the performance of their branches and strengthen the development of pro-agro service mechanisms. As for rural credit unions, village banks and other agro-related financial institutions, a flexible loan-to-deposit requirement was

applied. The tolerance for non-performing agro-related loans was increased. The CBRC conducted thematic inspection on banking charges to identify and deal with unfair charges, thus reducing the funding costs of agro-related companies and protecting the lawful rights and interests of financial consumers in rural areas.

(2) Increasing the extension of agro-related loans. Agro-related banking institutions were encouraged to make separate plans for the extension of agro-related loans and properly delegate the power for loan approval. The CBRC made quarterly disclosure of agro-related loans extended by banking institutions. In 2014, agro-related loans maintained a sound momentum. As of end-2014, the balance of outstanding agro-related loans by banking institutions reached RMB23.6 trillion, with an increase of RMB3.0 trillion compared with the year beginning and a year-on-year growth of 13.0 percent, 4 percentage points higher than the average loan growth rate. In December 2014, the CBRC issued the *Guidelines on Strengthening Supervision over Agro-related Financial Service Mechanisms by Rural Commercial Banks,* aiming at establishing a long-term mechanism for rural commercial banks to support agro-related developments.

(3) Strengthening financial support for key agro-related areas. Firstly, efforts were made to strengthen the support for food production. In 2014, the Agriculture Development Bank of China (ADBC) extended RMB521.02 worth of loans supporting the purchase of 473.39 billion kilos of grains and 10.38 billion kilos of edible oil, and RMB50.14 billion worth of loans for cotton purchase. As of end-2014, the balance of outstanding loans by ADBC in support of the production, processing and circulation of grains and other major agricultural products stood at RMB1,486.25 billion. Secondly, more support was given to new-type agricultural players. The CBRC issued the *Guiding Opinions on Improving Financial Support to Scale Agricultural Production and Intensive Management* (Yin Jian Fa [2014] No. 38) jointly with the Ministry of Agriculture, aiming to establish a rural financial organization system, an operation and management system, a financial product system, a risk diversification system, a rural credit system and a policy support system in line with the development of modern agriculture. It also aimed to establish and improve a financial system in support of new-type agricultural production, operation and organization, and guide financial institutions to give more support to new-type agricultural players in terms of market position, resource allocation, product service and incentive measures, thus unleashing the potential of agriculture and accelerating the development of modern agriculture. Thirdly, support to farmland irrigation and water conservation projects was strengthened. The scope of pledges and repayment sources was expanded for water conservancy projects. Efforts were also made to develop new-type financing models for water conservancy projects. As of end-2014, the balance of outstanding loans by the CDB, ADBC and PSBC in support of farmland irrigation and water conservancy projects stood at RMB365.233 billion.

(4) Diversifying rural financial service providers. Efforts were made to steadily promote the development of township and village banks. As of end-2014, there were 1,153 village and township banks in China, 61.1% of which were based in central and western China. They extended 2,626,000 loans worth RMB1.62 trillion to 1,521,000 rural households and 277,000 MSEs, accounting for 80.6 percent of all loans extended by village and township banks. As for financial leasing companies mainly providing services for agro-related projects, the CBRC granted approvals to 2 agro-related financial leasing companies for business commencement and to another 3 for preparatory establishment. The balance of outstanding loans of financial leasing companies in the agriculture, forestry, husbandry and fishery sectors stood at RMB7.2 billion. Trust companies were guided to support the agro-related development. In 2014, they invested RMB140.6 billion in the agro-related sector. Efforts were also made to explore the development of new-type cooperation finance for

supporting the agro-related development. The CBRC submitted the **Report on Credit Cooperation of Farmer Cooperatives** to the State Council. It also issued the **Notice on Guiding and Regulating Rural Credit Cooperation** (Yin Jian Fa [2014] No. 43) and drafted the **Research Report on the Development of New-type Rural Cooperative Financial Organizations** jointly with the Ministry of Agriculture and All China Federation of Supply and Marketing Cooperatives.

(5) Increasing the coverage of basic financial services. Building on the fact that all towns in China had access to basic financial services and all towns in 24 provinces enjoyed presence of financial institutions, the CBRC issued the **Guiding Opinions on Promoting Villages' Access to Financial Services**, guiding small and medium-sized rural financial institutions to strengthen financial services for rural areas and promote the innovation of financial products and services. They flexibly adopted diversified means to extend basic financial services at village level, facilitated the deployment of POS machines and ATM facilities, standard outlets and simplified outlets and expanded the service scope and contents via telephone banking, cellphone banking and other low-cost means, thus removing all access barriers to basic financial services. 520,000 administrative villages in China now enjoy access to financial services.

(6) Overall arrangements for rural financial services in 2014 were made to continuously promote three "major projects". In 2014, the CBRC submitted a request to the State Council for convening the National (Video) Conference for Sharing Rural Financial Service Experiences. The State Council concurrently issued the **Opinions of the State Council General Office on Providing Financial Services to Support the Agro-related Development** (Guo Ban Fa [2014] No. 17), setting out future directions and policy measures concerning rural financial development. The CBRC issued the **Notice on Improving Financial Services in 2014**, specifying the arrangements and requirements for banking institutions in providing rural financial services. In April, the CBRC issued the **Notice on Boosting Small and Medium-sized Rural Financial Institutions' Agro-Supporting Services for "Three Major Projects"** (Yin Jian Ban Fa [2014] No. 98). In September, an Experience Sharing Meeting on "Three Major Projects" was organized. The CBRC guided small and medium-sized rural financial institutions to improve the level of financial inclusion in rural areas, extend the openness of services to village level, strengthen the transparency and fairness in the management of the agro-lending process, increase financial support to new-type agricultural players, effectively promote micro-lending techniques and industrial chain financing, explore the development of mortgage loans secured by rural land contract management rights, homestead use rights, and farmers' housing property rights, and actively develop innovative financial products and services tailored to the needs of agro-related development.

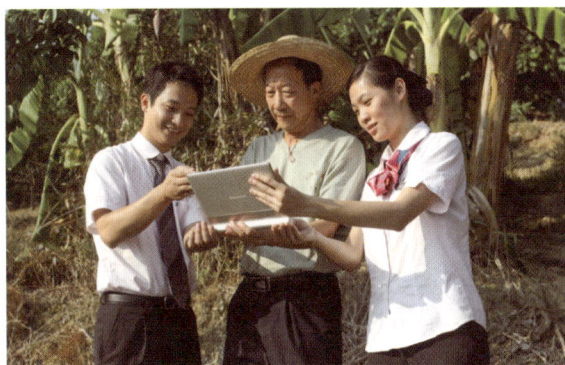

Credit officers of the PSBC Fujian Branch used mobile devices to provide on-site business service.

The PSBC provided micro-credit services to agro-related developments, helping growers shake off poverty.

Box 13　Promoting rural financial development and unleashing vitality

In 2014, the CBRC took a variety of measures to deepen the reform of small and medium-sized rural financial institutions, strengthen the development of the service mechanisms for agro-related undertakings, and stimulate the vitality of small and medium-sized rural financial institutions, thus effectively promoting rural financial development.

Firstly, private investors were encouraged to participate in the ownership reform of rural credit cooperatives. In order to implement the requirement of the State Council on encouraging, guiding and expanding private investment in the financial industry, the CBRC issued the ***Notice on Encouraging and Guiding Private Capital to Participate in the Ownership Reform of Rural Credit Cooperatives***, allowing rural credit cooperatives to introduce private capital for optimized ownership structure and improved corporate governance. The effort to develop eligible market players was accelerated, thereby upgrading the capabilities of rural banks to deliver better services for agro-related undertakings.

Secondly, policies for steadily developing village and township banks were improved. The CBRC issued the ***Guiding Opinions on Further Promoting the Healthy Development of Village and Township Banks***. Adhering to the requirement on minimum stake proportion of principal initiating bank, the CBRC followed the principles of financial risk prevention, financial service expansion and corporate governance improvement, and made efforts to further motivate banking institutions to collectively initiate the establishment of village and twonship banks, intensify the effort to introduce private capital, steadily boost full coverage of these banks in counties and cities, and thereby further improve the rural financial service system. It also boosted the localization, privatization and specialization of village and township banks, so as to improve distinct financial services for MSEs and agro-related undertakings.

Thirdly, the agro-supporting service mechanism was improved in line with the market orientation of agro-related development. The CBRC issued the ***Supervisory Guidelines on Strengthening Institutional Development of Financial Services to Agro-related Development by Rural Commercial Banks***, guiding rural commercial banks (rural cooperation banks and rural credit cooperatives) to strengthen the concept of financial inclusion, and improve the institutional arrangements in support of agro-related development in the areas of ownership structure, corporate governance, development strategy, organizational structure, business development, risk management, human resource, performance appraisal and supervisory evaluation.

◎ The CBRC Fujian Office disseminated Sha County's experiences in enhancing rural financial service

Sha county achieved breakthroughs in improving rural financial services through such innovative practices as improving rural credit evaluation mechanism, originating village-level financing guarantee fund, engaging industrial guarantee companies for credit enhancement, exploring rural housing loans, innovating land-transfer loans, implementing the "financial services within the village" program and establishing private capital management company, etc.. In 2014, the CBRC Fujian Office disseminated the rural financial reform experiences of Sha County in an extensive manner and introduced the experiences via teleconference on the sharing of rural financial services held by the State Council.

◎ The CBRC Guangxi Office promoted the full coverage of financial self-service terminals in the administrative villages of its jurisdiction

Under the guidance of the CBRC Guangxi Office, outstanding achievements of financial inclusion have been made by rural cooperative financial institutions. 24,944 sets of electronic devices named "GUI-SHENG-TONG" have been installed across the province, which provide services of small cash deposits and withdrawals, consumption fees payment, money transfers, agent payments, enquiries and etc. 4,931 sets of self-service terminals included ATM also have been installed, of which 2,942 sets of terminals were installed in villages and towns.

◎ The CBRC Hunan Office promoted the building of "One-County Two-Banks" system

Based on local reality, the CBRC Hunan Office put forward the idea of "One-County Two-Banks", which means making rural credit cooperatives be restructured to Rural Commercial Bank, and building one Rural Bank in each county. The CBRC Hunan Office has been taking the measures of "Two Tilts", namely, putting more regulatory resources and management resources into the equity reform of rural credit cooperatives,

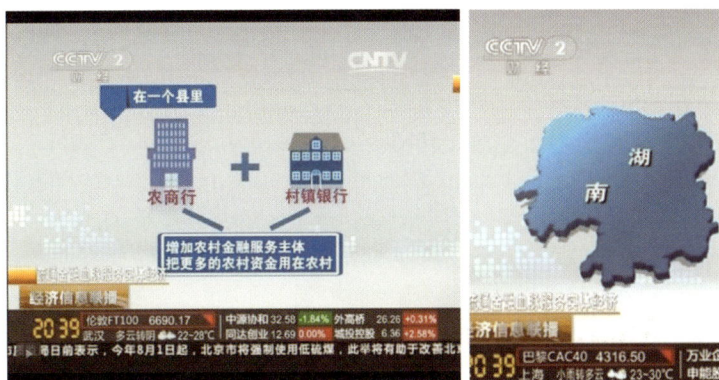

Economic information news.

"Two Emphases", namely, high-risk institution restructuring and urban institution integrating, and "Three Bundling", namely, the bundling of equity reform of RCCs with senior executives performance evaluation, with the annual performance assessment of CBRC sub-offices and their heads, and with the introduction of external financial institutions. Meanwhile, series of comprehensive measures were taken to promote collection, market absorption and government support with the aim to better handle the non-performing assets and fiscal burdens, promote equity reform of RCCs, nurture village and township banks, enrich the county financial services system, and increase financial services supply in countes. Hence, farmers production, shareholder's efficiency, and local government income could be increased.

◎ The CBRC Tibet Office promoted the development of rural cash service point and the deployment of ATM in rural area

2,472 rural cash service points were deployed in Tibet, with covered towns and administrative village registering 631 and 1,951 respectively. As of end 2014, 1,053 service spots for cash withdrawal were newly added for farmers, making the covered towns and administrative village of such services increased to 92.4 percent and 37.1 percent respectively. The financial institutions in Tibet recruited a total of 686 new employees, with 61.8 percent of new employees assigned to work in the rural area, thus largely solved the problem of a lack of employees in rural financial service spots and low mobility of financial services.

◎ The CBRC Zhejiang Office boosted supply chain finance in agricultural scale production and intensive management

The agricultural supply chain finance program was conducted in 24 pilot banks in Zhejiang province, with the focus on fostering the information, product and service chain along credit service to extend agro-related financial services from one individual debtor to a "chain" of integrated service, thus realizing an integrated solution of credit risk control, effective guarantee and promotion of agricultural scale production and intensive management. By the end of 2014, the pilot banks have offered about 30 target products and 6 service patterns covering the top 10 Zhejiang provincial agricultural leading industries and 40 subdivisions. Take Songyang Rural Credit Cooperatives Union as example, loan demands of tea chain farmers were estimated according to

Credit officer of Zhejiang Songyang Rural Credit Union visiting the tea growers.

basic source data, including, net income per acre multiplies acreage, the machine starts and monthly shipments. Its tea chain loan reached RMB260 million in 2014, benefiting over 2,000 tea farmers.

◎ The CBRC Qinghai Office pushed forward inclusive financial system with full coverage of financial services at counties and townships

The CBRC Qinghai office guided banking institutions to fill the blank of financial services through technologies and other convenient facilities. By installing money transfer telephones, POS machines, self-service terminals and providing mobile services, effective financial services were made available to remote agricultural and pastoral areas and unbanked villages and towns. In 2014, 742 sets of POS machines, 1,724 sets of electronic devices, and 1,685 agriculture-supporting service outlets were provided in unbanked villages and towns. Thus, all counties and townships in Qinghai province have gained access to financial services.

◎ The CBRC Gansu Office actively guided the banking insitutions to expand service channels in pastoral areas

The CBRC Gansu Office guided the banking industry under its jurisdiction to expand services in pastoral areas of Gannan Tibetan Autonomous Prefecture, such as offering mobile services in remote farming village by using mobile service vehicles.

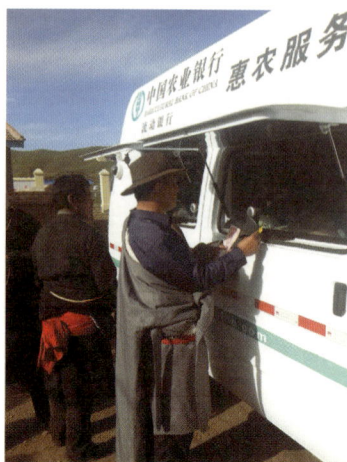

◎ Full coverage of telephone banking achieved in Hubei's administrative villages

In order to improve coverage of rural financial service, the CBRC Hubei Office made great efforts to promote full coverage of telephone banking. Firstly, it monitored and compiled statistics of telephone banking in the rural areas on a quarterly basis. Secondly, it urged banking institutions providing agro-related services within the jurisdiction to upgrade capabilities of telephone banking, while at the same time promoting non-cash settlement in the rural areas. Thirdly, it strengthened incentive mechanism and supervisory evaluation mechanism, which link the deployment of telephone banking with supervisory evaluation and link the local supervisory guidance with annual assessment. As of end 2014, telephone banking was made available to 25,554 administrative villages of Hubei Province. 98,965 units of telephone banking were installed, up by 32.4 percent from year beginning. The amount of yearly transactions through telephone banking facility registered RMB13.897 million, up by 43.4 percent year-on-year, while transaction value reached RMB121.9 billion, up by 74.8 percent year-on-year.

◎ Agricultural Development Bank of China served agricultural cultivation and supported agriculture, rural area and farmers

Agricultural Development Bank of China provided RMB410 million to support the high standard farmland demonstration project in Hailar, and helped remould 336 thousand mu of high standard farmland. The land utilization rate therefore increased by 7 percent, and grain and edible oil production increased by 60,480 tons per year. The efforts have resulted in a dynamic integration of increased agricultural output, enterprise efficiency and farm workers' income.

Wheat harvest at Haila'er, Inner Mongolia.

3. Financial services for communities

With a view to promoting people's livelihood and protecting consumers' rights and interests, the CBRC encouraged small and medium-sized commercial banks to provide financial services for local communities, while strengthening regulation and guidance for those banks to set reasonable layout and realize full compliance, so as to avoid disorderly vicious competition and illegal operations.

As of end-2014, small and medium-sized commercial banks set up 2,840 community sub-branches and 480 micro and small-sized sub-branches. The CBRC continued to regulate and guide community sub-branches. The licensing process was simplified to support the development of community sub-branches and micro and small-sized sub-branches. Specialized sub-branches already approved were encouraged to stay committed to serving community residents and MSEs, implement the regulatory requirements on licensed operations and information disclosure, and improve the specialized service level.

> ## ◎ Banking institutions in Jilin province strengthened community financial services

The CBRC Jilin Office promoted joint-stock commercial banks in its jurisdiction to enhance financial services at grassroot level, including the establishment of community branches and micro and small branches to better serve the neighboring communities in 2014. It approved the establishment of 24 community branches and 6 micro and small branches by joint-stock commercial banks. By the end of 2014, 13 community branches and 1 micro and small branch had been approved, while 3 community branches and 2 micro and small branches were in the process of preparation for establishment.

Media perspective 4   The CBRC established the Financial Inclusion Affairs Department to guide the sound development of P2P lending

On January 20, the CBRC announced that it had officially launched the first major organizational restructuring since 2003. Existing 27 departments were split and merged into 23 departments, including 22 administrative functions and 1 government sponsored institution. The most eye-catching aspect of the reform was the establishment of the Financial Inclusion Affairs Department responsible for supervising P2P lending related affairs.

Before restructuring, P2P lending was subject to no entry requirements, no industrial standards and no supervisory authorities. The number of both new entrants and problematic platforms was increasing sharply. The number of platform problems occurring in December 2013 was almost equal to the total in the previous 11 months. After experiencing such things as "staking out turf" and "fly-by-night operators", some serious P2P operators lobbied hard for regulations.

The new Financial Inclusion Affairs Department is said to consist of the Office of the Steering Group for Improving Financial Services for SMEs, the Rural Financial Services Supervision Division, the Financing Guarantee Division, the newly-established Micro Credit Companies Association and P2P Lending Supervision Division. The CBRC said that the restructuring provided overall arrangements for the delivery and supervision of financial services, and great efforts would be made to promote financial inclusion. In the spirit of putting people first in supervision, the Financial Inclusion Affairs Department will focus its efforts on promoting financial services for MSEs, agro-related development and other under-banked areas, and strengthening the supervisory coordination among unlicensed micro credit companies, P2P lending companies, and financing guarantee companies.

Along with the boom of Internet finance, the CBRC has placed P2P lending and other Internet finance practices under the financial inclusion supervision in the hope of guiding the sound development of Internet finance.

(Source: excerpted from: finance.ifeng.com)

IV. Addressing overcapacity and promoting green credit

1. Improving regulatory policies and strengthening policy guarantee

In 2014, the CBRC issued the *Guiding Opinions on Supporting Industrial Restructuring and Addressing Overcapacity* with a view to guiding banking institutions to support the expansion of reasonable credit demands to absorb some capacities, support companies to "go global" to transfer some capacities, support companies in mergers and restructuring to consolidate some capacities, and strengthen the liquidation protection to phase out some capacities. Following the principle of differentiated treatment, banking institutions were guided to develop and implement differentiated credit policies aligned with China's national economic development strategies, and boost the industrial upgrading and transformation by developing and executing

Vice Chairman WANG Zhaoxing attended the China Banking Development Forum.

credit classification criteria and promoting green credit. In addition, the CBRC issued the ***Guiding Opinions on Strengthening NPL Prevention and Control in 2014***, requiring banking institutions to support the development of real economy while controlling credit risks. As for overcapacity industries and other key areas, banks were required to adopt differentiated credit policies and avoid withdrawing, stopping or suspending loans in an one-size-fits-all manner which might cause rupture of companies' capital chain as a result .

2. Strengthening risk monitoring and supervision

The mechanism for monitoring credit risks of overcapacity industries was established. The policy concerning the statistics of loans in key industries as well as the statistics of green loans was developed and improved. The CBRC also monitored the loans to "industries with high pollution, high energy consumption and overcapacities", watched the risks of key corporate clients, group clients, affiliates and co-guarantee clients, and gave risk alerts to banking institutions when appropriate. The CBRC also made field trips to regions with concentrated overcapacities to understand the credit and risk profiles of relevant industries. Based on the findings, the CBRC gave risk alerts and business guidance to banking institutions in a timely manner. As of end-2014, the loans outstanding of 21 major banks to overcapacity industries, including steel and iron, cement, plate glass, aluminum smelting, metal shipbuilding, stood at RMB1.03 trillion, with their share out of total loans dropping by 0.3 percentage point compared with the year beginning.

3. Promote green credit to support energy conservation and environmental protection

Banking institutions were encouraged to support key national energy-efficient projects, key environmental protection projects and technological upgrading or renovation projects using advanced energy-efficient technologies. They were also encouraged to step up support to energy conservation, emission reduction and environmental protection, and actively support industrial restructuring and corporate technological upgrading or renovation. As of end-2014, the balance of green credit loans extended by 21 major banks totaled RMB6.01 trillion, up 15.67 percent over the year beginning and accounting for 9.33 percent of all loans. The projects with green credit support were expected to achieve the following results, including, coal consumption reduced by 167 million tons of standard coal; water consumption reduced by 934 million tones; CO_2 emission reduced by 400 million tons, SO_2 emission reduced by 5,876,500 tons, COD reduced by 3.413,000 tons, nitrogen oxide reduced by 1,600,900 tons, and ammonia nitrogen reduced by 340,800 tons.

Box 14   The CBRC issued the *Key Performance Indicators for Implementing Green Credit*

In June, the CBRC issued the **Key Performance Indicators for Implementing Green Credit** (hereinafter referred to as the KPI), guiding banking institutions to conduct self-evaluation so that they could effectively incorporate the green credit concept into banking operations, increase the awareness of extending green credit to boost the ecological development, actively develop innovative green financial products, and give more support to green economy, circular economy and low-carbon economy. The KPI includes both qualitative and quantitative indicators. Qualitative indicators define the goals and evaluation standards banking institutions shall meet in terms of the roles and responsibilities of the board of directors, senior management's roles and responsibilities, centralized management, policy development, classified management, green innovation, business performance, capacity building, due diligence, compliance review, credit approval, contract administration, fund transfer management, post-loan management, management of overseas projects, internal control examination, appraisal and evaluation, information disclosure, and self assessment. Quantitative indicators cover four aspects, i.e. loan extension to supported and restricted projects, operating environment and social performance, green credit training and education, and interaction with stakeholders.

◎ Banking institutions actively supported air pollution control in Beijing, Tianjin and Hebei

Banks in Beijing, Tianjin and Hebei implemented differentiated credit policies and developed green credit to help companies phase out backward capacities and realize transformation and upgrading, and support biomass power and renewable energy projects, so as to control air pollution. As of end-2014, the outstanding loans to "industries with high pollution, high energy consumption and overcapacities" stood at RMB458.367 billion, up 6.69 percent year on year, and the outstanding loans to energy saving and emission reduction projects, circular economy projects and other environmental protection projects and services stood at RMB889.956 billion, up 27.07 percent year on year. The ABC innovated and promoted the factoring business for the beneficiary right of energy saving and emission reduction projects. The Industrial Bank developed 7 special products, such as carbon asset pledged financing. The BOCom extended RMB1 billion worth of loans to support 11 biomass power projects.

◎ The CBRC Guizhou Office strengthened monitoring and resolution of risks associated with overcapacity industries

The CBRC Guizhou Office set up a monitoring, analysis and reporting mechanism, a credit risk warning system against key enterprises and a resolution system against key enterprises facing difficulties. It implemented differentiated policies on different overcapacity industries. It also regularly convened meetings of creditor banks and relevant authorities overseeing respective industries to discuss risk conditions of key industries and enterprises and put forward countermeasures.

◎ The CBRC Liaoning Office implemented credit limit on enterprises violating environmental policies in conjunction with related departments

The CBRC Liaoning Office, together with Department of Environmental Protection of Liaoning Province, and the People's Bank of China Shenyang Branch, strictly implemented the green credit policy on 25 environmental offenders in glass, cement, steel, thermal power, textile industries, such as Shenyang Zhong Nan Thermal Power Co., Ltd., etc.. According to relevant policy, in principle all banking institutions within Liaoning's jurisdiction should not issue new loans to those environmental offenders, and gradually cut down loans until the final exit in accordance with the actual circumstances.

◎ Industrial Bank strengthened specialized operations to build green financial industrial chain

As the first and only Equator Bank in China, the Industrial Bank exclusively created the carbon asset risk management and Assessment Value model (AV model), invented the first domestic carbon pledge product, accomplished the first national agent bank account system of the carbon trading system, signed the cooperation agreements with 6 national carbon trading pilots, completed the first green financial asset backed securitization project. By the end of 2014, the Industrial Bank had provided RMB555.8 billion supporting green finance business for thousands of companies, while the financing balance of green finance of the entire bank stood at RMB 296 billion, an increase of RMB 114.8 billion from the beginning of 2014. The Industrial Bank green finance business covers three main areas, including low carbon economy, circular economy, and ecological economy.

V. Fully promoting balanced regional development

1. Central and western regions

In order to develop and improve financial system in the central and western regions, the CBRC guided banking institutions to adjust regional credit allocation, and therefore improved the unbalanced allocation of credit resources between underdeveloped and developed regions. As of end-2014, the growth of outstanding loans in the central and western regions was 4.7 percentage points higher than that in the eastern region. The top 10 provinces with the highest growth rate were Tibet (50.4 percent), Gansu (25.5 percent), Guizhou (22.5 percent), Qinghai (22.4 percent), Jiangxi (19.7 percent), Xinjiang (17.9 percent), Jilin (17.5 percent), Henan (17.3 percent), Heilongjiang (17.1 percent) and Ningxia (16.7 percent).

2. Old industrial bases in China's northeast region

Firstly, efforts were made to develop and improve the financial system in old industrial bases in China's northeast region. Eligible small and medium-sized banks were guided to improve their institutional network in China's northeast region, and local small and medium-sized banks were encouraged to give more support to under-banked

Disciplinary Commissioner DU Jinfu made a field trip to Heilongjiang.

areas. As for foreign banks that established operations in China's northeast region, green channel policies were implemented for encouraging and guiding them to set up offices and conduct business operations in the old industrial bases. Eligible investors were also encouraged to set up non-bank institutions. Efforts were made to strengthen the building of financial service capacity in rural areas and boost the development of village and township banks and rural commercial banks.

Secondly, banking institutions were encouraged and guided to strengthen credit support. The 5 major banks were encouraged to increase their support for the steady and sound economic development in China's northeast region and allocate more credit resources for this region. Small and medium-sized banks were guided to focus on infrastructure, agro-related and livelihood-related projects, and intensify efforts to provide financial services for MSEs. Non-bank institutions were encouraged to give more support for key localities, areas, industries and clients in old industrial bases in China's northeast region. Rural small and medium financial innovations were encouraged to provide more innovative agro-related financial products and services.

◎ The CBRC Dalian Office supported the revitalization of the old northeast industrial base and construction of JinPu national new district

In 2014, the State Council approved the establishment of Dalian JinPu District and issued the opinion about a number of major recent policies to support the revitalization of the Northeast. In accordance with the actual situations of Dalian, the CBRC Dalian office conducted an in-depth study of the policies, and issued the opinions about twelve aspects, including, playing the function of financing effectively, optimizing the allocation of financial resources, reducing the cost of funding the real economy, etc.. With these measures, Dalian banking industry were guided to play an active role in the revitalization of the Northeast old industrial base and construction of JinPu new district.

3. Xinjiang autonomous region

Firstly, the CBRC promoted the development of the banking system. Banking institutions were guided to optimize their institutional outlets and services, and increase the coverage of outlets and services in Xinjiang, especially in southern Xinjiang. The CBRC facilitated the preparations for the establishment of Xinjiang Bank, and granted approval to China Minsheng Bank for the establishment of its Urumqi Branch. The Yili Branch of the Industrial Bank has commenced operations. Besides, 7 rural commercial banks has commenced operations, while 18 village and township banks, 75 banking outlets were established, and 29 community sub-branches commenced business in Xinjiang. In addition, the CBRC actively encouraged policy banks and large banks to set up more offices in southern Xinjiang. The banking business and operations began to take shape in Kashgar Economic Development Zone and Khorgos Economic Development Zone.

Secondly, differentiated supervisory polices and preferential credit policies were adopted to encourage banking institutions to give more credit support for key projects, livelihood-related projects and weak areas in Xinjiang, aiming to improve local infrastructure development and public service delivery and further support Xinjiang's economic and social development. As of end-2014, the balance of outstanding loans extended by banking institutions in Xinjiang stood at RMB1.2 trillion, up 17.92 percent year on year and 4.62 percentage points higher than national average growth rate, ranking 6th nationwide.

Thirdly, banking institutions were guided to support the development of related projects, such as the Core Area of Silk Road Economic Belt, China-Pakistan Economic Corridor, China-Pakistan Railway, China-Kirgizstan Railway, etc., and give more financial support to the economic development zones of Kashgar and Khorgos.

4. Tibet

To support the development of Tibet, the CBRC guided banking institutions to optimize their outlet layout, and strengthen credit support for key projects, agro-related undertakings, MSEs and weak areas, thus stimulating the growth of local economy. Firstly, the Workshop on Encouraging Banking Institutions to Support Tibet's Economic and Social Development was held, so as to motivate banks to adopt preferential policies and set up offices in Tibet, thereby driving the development of the banking sector in Tibet. Secondly, the CBRC guided transformation of banking operation models, boosted policy bank reform, and pushed locally incorporated banks to improve corporate governance. Thirdly, banks were encouraged to make financial innovations; as a result, more financial products were offered, including agency business, consultancy and evaluation business, investment and wealth management business, etc., and service approaches were expanded to include online banking, telephone banking, pro-farmers service center for deposit withdrawal , etc.. Fourthly, the financing needs in key areas were satisfied, supporting the development of a range of projects related to energy saving and emission reduction, independent innovation, structural adjustment, infrastructure, environmental protection and ecological improvement. Fifthly, financial services for weak areas were improved. In Tibet, the balance of outstanding ago-related loans stood at RMB29.726 billion, with an increase of RMB14.72 billion or 98.09 percent year on year. The growth rate was 7.7 times that of the national average. The annual target of RMB20 billion loan extension was achieved ahead of schedule. Over 350,000 rural households obtained loans. The balance of outstanding loans to MSEs stood at RMB25.8 billion, with an increase of RMB6.6 billion or 34.6 percent year on year. Sixthly, inclusive financial services became widely extended. The establishment of pro-farmers service center for deposit withdrawal and installation of self-service machines increased the coverage of financial services and improved the equal access to financial services in towns.

Photograph by the CBRC staff

Part Four

CBRC
Annual Report
2014

Enhancing Law-based Regulation to Strengthen Supervisory Capability

- Building Supervisory Framework
- Supervisory approaches
- Supervisory cooperation and coordination
- Organizational development

I. Building Supervisory Framework

1. Enhancing regulatory legal framework

In 2014, the CBRC improved the regulatory legal framework to provide sufficient legal protection for banking regulation. The CBRC issued six regulations including the *Rules on Service Charges of Commercial Banks,* the *Rules on Liquidity Risk Management of Commercial Banks (Provisional),* the *Rules governing Financial Leasing Companies,* the *Implementation Rules on Administrative Licensing of Small- and Medium-sized Financial Institutions in Rural Areas,* the *Provisional Rules on Factoring Business of Commercial Banks* and the *Implementation Rules on Administrative Licensing of Foreign-funded Banks*, and participated in drafting or amending laws and regulations, such as the *Provisional Regulations on Cash Management,* the *Interim Measures for the Regulation of Privately Offered Investment Funds* and the *Interim Regulation on Real Estate Registration*.

2. Improving rules for prudential supervision

In 2014, the CBRC regulated banking businesses such as interbank business and wealth management business, and strengthened regulation on deposit deviation degree, loan-to-deposit ratio and internal controls, so as to improve rules for prudential supervision. The CBRC formulated and issued 14 regulatory documents including the *Notice of the CBRC General Office on Regulating Interbank Business of Commercial Banks,* the *Notice of the CBRC on Improving the System for the Organization and Management of Wealth Management Business,* the *Notice of the CBRC on Adjusting Loan-to-Deposit Ratio Calculation Methods for Commercial Banks, Notice of the General Office of the CBRC, the General Office of the Ministry of Finance and the General Office of the People's Bank of China (PBC) Concerning Strengthening the Administration of Deposit Deviation Degree of Commercial Banks* and the *Guidelines on Internal Controls of Commercial Banks.*

3. Streamlining administration and delegating power

In 2014, the CBRC promoted reform on administrative licensing and approval system, reduced approval items to optimize approval procedure; meanwhile, the CBRC strengthened in-process and follow-up management to make supervision more effective and safeguard the bottom line of preventing

Vice Chairman YAN Qingmin made a field trip to Ningxia.

regional or systemic risks. Three out of the 12 approval items were abolished, which met the required cut-down ratio. The CBRC publicized all the existing administrative licensing and approval items and approved projects, putting its power under the supervision of banking financial institutions and the general public.

4. Clean-up and compiling regulatory policies on a full scale

In 2014, the CBRC did a full-scale clean-up of regulations and regulatory documents about the banking sector, and issued the *Review Results of Regulatory Documents* that lists 393 regulatory documents in effect and 139 abolished by the CBRC from its establishment and to the end of 2012. Based on the review results and published catalogue of regulatory policies, CBRC started compilation of existing regulatory policies.

Box 15   Promoting law-based regulation in the banking sector

Since the reform and opening up, especially since the liberalization of the market economy, the CBRC has been promoting law-based regulation in the banking sector, providing legal guarantee for the banking reform, regulation and development. During more than 30 years of banking reform and development, the law-based regulation has been advanced, strengthened and deepened.

1. A preliminary legal framework that fits into China's banking development was set up. First, building a modern banking system now has basic legal grounds. From the *Provisional Regulations on Banking Regulation* in 1986, to the *Law on Commercial Banks* in 1995 and its revision in 2003, China's banking system has transformed from a centralized one in the planned economy to a more diversified sector made up of modern commercial banks in the market economy. During this process, each major step has been guided, reaffirmed and consolidated by laws and regulations. Second, strengthening banking regulation has gained legitimacy. From initial administrative provisions to the *Law on People's Bank of China* and then the *Banking Supervision Law*, banking regulation has clearer objectives and responsibilities with more effective measures and extensive expertise. Third, rules relevant to the banking sector have been improved. *Negotiable Instruments Law, Guarantee Law, Contract Law, Trust Law* and *Property Law* among others were introduced and are serving as legal basis for regulating transaction of related parties and protecting stakeholders in the banking sector.

2. A prudential supervision system was formed. Since its establishment, the CBRC has been pursuing risk-based supervision and has formulated and issued a number of rules for prudential supervision. As of the end of 2014, 48 regulations and more than 400 regulatory documents were in effect, which formed a complete system of supervisory rules. In business management, major businesses including deposits, loans, interbank business, wealth management products, bankcards and derivatives all have rules to follow. In institutional management, requirements are in place for corporate governance, performance evaluation, internal control, external audit, etc.. In risk management, capital management, credit risks, market risks, operational risks, and liquidity risks are put under regulations. In supervisory practice, regulations throughout the whole regulatory process including licensing, off-site surveillance, on-site examination and market exit were developed.

3. A comprehensive and coherent legal work system was built. First, with respect to the organizational structure, the Legal Department was set up at the CBRC head office with the previous functions of handling illegal fundraising, financial innovation supervision and policy research removed in order to focus on legal work; meanwhile, specialized legal divisions were also set up in the CBRC provincial offices. Second, a number of qualified legal experts joined the CBRC to provide their expertise. Currently, more than 700 staff are working in the legal area at the CBRC, of which over one third have obtained master's degree. This professional legal team have played a vital role in promoting law-based supervision. Third, a complete system for legal work is in place. The CBRC issued basic work provisions such as *Provisions on the Legal Work*

of the CBRC, and established the system of legal review and filing review of regulations and regulatory policies. The CBRC set up review and compilation system that requires regulations to be cleaned up every five years, and regulatory documents, every two years, in order to keep regulatory policies up-to-date.

4.A multi-tiered system of international cooperation and inter-agency coordination was built. First, the CBRC strengthened international supervisory cooperation by signing MOUs with regulatory authorities of more than 60 jurisdictions, participated in rule-making process of the Basel Committee on Banking Supervision (BCBS), held a number of bilateral and multilateral talks to strengthen the international supervisory cooperation in a formal and regular manner. Second, the CBRC improved coordination with local governments and judiciary departments. The CBRC has been facilitating the coordination between supervisory enforcement and judicial execution, promoted to speed up the trial, judgment and execution process of banking cases, helped to handle the resolution of major financial debt risks according to the law, cracked down on companies' evasion of debt payment and therefore effectively protected financial claims and maintained the market order. Third, the CBRC strengthen financial supervisory coordination by actively participating in the financial supervisory coordination mechanism, and working with the securities and insurance supervisory agencies to effectively prevent contagion of cross-sector risks.

◎ **The CBRC Qingdao Office launched the regular review mechanism of rules and regulations**

Firstly, an internal review mechanism was established. The CBRC Qingdao Office conducted revision and supplementation work of rules and regulations internally in a forward-looking manner since 2013, which sorted out 141 effective documents and led to the establishment of a regular review mechanism. It also piloted the working mechanism of administrative lawsuit, legal consultation and examination and penalty commission etc.. Secondly, the CBRC Qingdao Office strictly executed the working mechanism of clearing up regulatory documents biennially. Following the clear-up, 43 regulatory documents were deemed effective while 14 were made invalid in 2014, with the clear-up results announced publicly to banking institutions in Dalian.

II. Supervisory approaches

1.Licensing

(1)Following the principle of streamlining administration and delegating power, the CBRC streamlined administrative and approval items and optimized the approval procedure. First, the CBRC has been improving related regulations, and issued the *Notice on Further Streamlining Administration and Delegating Power to Improve Market Entry,* revised and issued the *Implementation Rules on Administrative Licensing of Small- and Medium-sized Financial Institutions in Rural Areas,* and renewed licensing procedures for non-bank financial institutions. Second, the CBRC changed supervisory approaches to combine "delegation of power" and "enhancing supervision". While prudently lowering administrative licensing requirement and simplifying administrative terms, the CBRC has taken the advantage of licensing as the frontline of risk prevention and strengthened in-process and follow-up supervision to strike a balance between "power delegation" and "effective supervision" and avoid supervisory gaps.

(2)Following the principle of financial inclusion, the CBRC guided banks to optimize their geographical presence so as to promote balanced economic and financial development among regions. The CBRC guided large commercial banks to expand their business units towards northeastern and central western regions, and also required these banks to follow the principle of financial inclusion in setting their annual plan for adding new business units so as to improve their capacity of providing inclusive services. The CBRC supported eligible

Vice Chairman CAO Yu made a field trip to the Bank of Beijing.

small- and medium-sized commercial banks, based on their commercial and voluntary actions, to set up outlets in remote or underdeveloped areas, supported Xinjiang province to improve financial service system, supported foreign banks to open outlets in northeastern and central western regions, and gave preferential policies to foreign banks with managerial expertise and comparative advantages in financial service for agriculture, small- and micro-sized enterprises, and financing for commodities and ships to set up outlets in China; supported Hong Kong banks to set up outlets in Guangdong province in the form of sub-branches outside Hong Kong; strengthened support of policy finance for agricultural and rural development; issued the *Guiding Opinions on Further Promoting the Healthy Development of Village and Township Banks* and supported setting up village and township banks in underdeveloped areas, major agricultural areas and locations with clusters of MSEs and raising coverage ratio of village and township banks in counties and towns; the CBRC guided medium- and small-sized rural financial institutions to deliver service down to the areas where lack access to financial services, issued the *Notice on Strengthening Small- and Medium-sized Financial Institution Network in Rural Areas*, encouraged them to set up more outlets in rural communities and urban-rural continuum, and encouraged eligible rural commercial banks to set up outlets in underdeveloped counties within their respective provinces.

(3)Based on the principle of encouraging innovation, the CBRC promoted reform and innovation in the banking sector to better serve the real economy. The CBRC supported large commercial banks and financial asset management companies to build up their network in Shanghai Free Trade Zone (SFTZ). The CBRC encouraged the innovation of green credit, agricultural and rural related products, and credit products for small enterprises that directly serve the real economy so that credit funding can be allocated to sectors and enterprises in urgent need of the fund. The CBRC participated in formulating the plan of deepening reform on the China Development Bank, and approved its move to set up the Residential Housing Finance Department. The CBRC prudently expanded pilot programs of comprehensive businesses operation for small- and medium-sized commercial banks, promoted consumer finance companies to expand pilot programs so as to upgrade residential consumption and industries in urban and rural areas. The CBRC encouraged foreign banks to leverage their

Supervisors were analyzing off-site surveillance data.

advantages and experience from parent banks to innovate businesses. The CBRC encouraged pilot programs of credit asset securitization, and guided banking financial institutions to engage in the capital instrument innovation. The CBRC also encouraged rural small- and medium-sized financial institutions to issue special financial bonds for agriculture, farmers and rural areas.

2.Off-site surveillance

(1)The off-site surveillance system was improved. The CBRC optimized the off-site surveillance reporting form system and cut down the number of reporting forms, implemented new statistical system of client risk on full-scale, revised the **Guidelines on Consolidated Administration and Supervision on Commercial Banks** to guide commercial banks to improve the framework and model of consolidated management. The CBRC also issued **Guidelines on Supervisory Ratings of Commercial Banks** to make supervisory ratings more precise and accurate.

(2)Data quality was improved. The CBRC issued the **Notice on Further Improving the Quality of Regulatory Statistical Data,** the **Notice on the Establishment of the Quality Commitment System for Key Off-Site Regulatory Indicator Data** and the **Notice on Implementing the Management Criteria for Banking Statistical Information in Rural Cooperative Financial Institutions**, as ongoing efforts to promote the establishment of data quality supervision system and improve data quality management.

(3)The off-site surveillance toolkit was enriched. First, the CBRC introduced more risk analysis tools, upgraded early warning system of bank risks, promoted application of warning system of client risks, pushed ahead with stress testing, compiled the **Manual for Stress Testing** and issued the **Guidelines on Stress Testing of Commercial Banks**. Second, the CBRC studied about and built a new "toolkit for risk supervision and management of commercial banks" to make analysis tools for off-site surveillance more scientific. Third, the CBRC explored differentiated supervisory measures and introduced targeted measures for foreign banks, China Development Banks, etc., so as to balance both supervision and growth.

(4)Off-site surveillance coordination was strengthened. The CBRC continued to strengthen coordination with related parties to form concerted efforts. Departments in the CBRC head office jointly reviewed approval items, departments and offices cooperated in supervising comprehensive businesses of banking institutions, the CBRC head office and provincial offices jointly worked on supervisory coordination platform, and the CBRC worked with overseas regulatory authorities to hold international supervisory colleges.

(5)International cooperation was intensified. The CBRC actively participated in the international supervisory statistical reform, improved China's statistics modules and reporting requirement for international quantitative impact studies, organized banks to conduct quantitative impact studies for Basel III, and completed data reporting of global systemically important banks.

Box 16   The CBRC issued the *Guidelines on Supervisory Ratings of Commercial Banks*

In June 2014, the CBRC issued the ***Guidelines on Supervisory Ratings of Commercial Banks*** ("the ***Guidelines***") and improved the supervisory rating system for commercial banks. The ***Guidelines*** dynamically reflects the changes in international and domestic supervisory rules, with adjustments in response to changes in business development and risk characteristics of China's commercial banks, which makes the supervisory rating system more comprehensive and forward-looking. Improvement was made in the following five aspects. First, rating elements were enriched and rating standards were updated, which led to a more comprehensive and accurate rating system. Second, indicator setting was improved, risk assessment results were utilized to make the new rating system more forward-looking

and dynamic. Third, indicator setting model was improved, and authorization of adjustment was given to make the new rating system more adaptive to differentiated supervision. Fourth, ratings were refined and rating procedure was optimized to make the new rating system more granular and comparative. Fifth, weighting in quantitative and qualitative studies were prudentially determined and the grading model was adjusted to better balance professional judgment and quantitative rating. To ensure the applicability of the ***Guidelines***, the CBRC conducted pilot ratings on a number of selected commercial banks, and the findings showed that the new rating system is more rigorous, and the rating results are more prudential and can better reflect banks' real situation.

◎ Development and application of stress testing system made new progress

The CBRC emphasized the combination of development and application of stress testing. In institutional development, following the latest international supervisory standards and considering the real situation of China's banking sector, the CBRC revised and issued the *Guidelines on Stress Testing in Commercial Banks* that guides the implementation of stress testing, which encourages commercial banks to improve their stress testing and apply the results in business development and risk management, etc.. The CBRC also strengthened the role of supervision in the stress testing system so that stress testing can really serve as an important tool in banking risk management and banking supervision. In practice, the CBRC organized 19 major banks to conduct a series of stress testing in 2014. For the first time, stress testing for overall credit risks combined both the top-down and bottom-up approaches, with various models verifying each other, the results of which were fully utilized in supervision.

3.On-site examination

(1)Key areas were identified to make the on-site examination more targeted. First, the CBRC insisted on risk-based approach by emphasizing on prominent issues and major risks such as credit risk, non-credit assets, off-balance sheet business, liquidity risk, operational risk, corporate governance and internal controls. Second, the CBRC conducted targeted and differentiated on-site examinations that focus on risks in different regions, institutions and businesses.

(2)Examination approaches were improved and coordination was strengthened. First, the CBRC led the on-site examination work and conducted 57 full-scale examinations regarding 63 small- and medium-sized commercial banks, carried out the coordinated examination on interest rate risk on banking book in foreign banks for the first time, organized 31 CBRC provincial offices to conduct on-site examinations on rural cooperative financial institutions regarding their internal controls effectiveness and asset quality. Second, the CBRC improved examination approaches by conducting on-site examinations on liability business of some large commercial banks, shifting the traditional focus on compliarc to projects and clients in order to grasp the substantive risks of projects, strengthening internal coordination to track the fund flow. Third, the ways of on-site examination were innovated with the major responsibility for examination and cross-checking separately assigned to different CBRC departments or local offices, and "micro-communication" platform for on-site examinations were utilized by using new social media technologies. Fourth, the EAST system was fully applied. In 2014, the CBRC carried out 329 examination analysis projects covering credit, bank papers, interbank businesses, wealth management, etc..

(3)Examination measures were intensified to improve effectiveness of on-site examinations. First, the CBRC arranged and carried out "two strengthening and two curbing" campaign to guard against financial risks. Second, the CBRC strengthened "six measures" and innovated "four mechanisms" to make on-site examinations more effective. The "six measures" are strengthening the effectiveness of EAST, administration on supervisors, control and evaluation of examination quality, supervision on and accountability of examinations, combination of examinations and field trips and coordination between on-site examinations and relevant activities. The "four mechanism" are appropriately promoting cross-examination mechanism, developing "four pools", establishing effective evaluation mechanism and building an information exchange platform.

(4)Follow-up work was carried out to track banks' correction progress. First, the CBRC insisted on follow-up work, examining and approving banks' correction measures through effectiveness assessment, substantive testing, and compliance test, etc.. Second, the CBRC focused on the correction progress of the banks found with major deficiencies before, and held discussions about the remedies in key areas with the senior management.

(5)Accountability was stepped up to keep high pressure on potential banking cases. The CBRC played the deterring role of on-site examinations, implemented the provisions of "holding directors of two ranks above accountable" in determining responsibilities, and established and improved the long-term mechanism of case prevention. The CBRC also used multiple measures such as administrative penalties, postponed licensing, lowered rating, business suspension, open criticism within the sector, and coordinated work in accountability to seriously handle activities against laws and regulations.

◎ The CBRC Heilongjiang Office further enhanced its on-site examination capability

The CBRC Heilongjiang Office improved the continuity and application of on-site examination techniques, methods and standards by setting up the on-site examination plans database, which standardized examination plans for similar projects. The irregularities database was also established. The CBRC Heilongjiang Office integrated its regulatory resources to strengthen its on-site examination capability and optimized the jointly examination mechanism with other financial regulatory authorities, field offices and auditing departments of banking institutions. Guiding Opinions were issued to improve the effectiveness and efficiency of corrective measures required following the on-site examinations, so as to curb similar problems from repeating. Meanwhile, the CBRC Heilongjiang Office strengthened systematic management of the field offices and strengthened quality control of on-site examination by effective organization, adequate performance evaluation and proper reporting.

Box 17   The CBRC deployed and carried out "two strengthening and two curbing" campaign

In December, the CBRC issued the *Notice on Comprehensively Strengthening Banking Supervision by Special Inspections on Banking Financial Institutions' Strengthening of Curbing of the Business Operations in violation of Regulations and Illegal and Criminal Activities* and the *Notice on Comprehensively Conducting Special Inspections on Banking Financial Institutions' Strengthening of Internal Management and Control and Curbing of the Business Operations in violation of Regulations and Illegal and Criminal Activities*. On December

5, the CBRC held the teleconference on "two strengthening and two curbing" to urge banking institutions to conduct self-examinations, strengthen internal controls, curb activities violating laws and regulations, and guard against financial risks. In 2015, the CBRC and its offices plan to conduct spot examinations on banking institutions. The CBRC will also conduct comprehensive self-examinations and remedies regarding "strengthening supervision, circumventing activities against laws and regulations" to improve the effectiveness of supervision.

Box 18   Examining the application of EAST

In 2014, the EAST system was applied throughout the CBRC, and collected 61.43 T of standardized data for supervision, including data of 54.3226 million corporate accounts and 3.242 billion other accounts. Under the guidance of CBRC, CBRC offices used EAST to conduct 329 examination analysis projects covering credit, bank notes, interbank businesses, wealth management products, prevention and control

of cases, client risks among other risks.

EAST was used to conduct big data mining and analysis for identifying common and idiosyncratic cases in risk trends and management of banking institutions, so as to provide important basis for supervisory decision-making to hold the bottom-line of guarding against systemic and regional risks.

Box 19   Key on-site examination projects

Large commercial banks: on-site examinations on off-balance-sheet businesses of the ICBC and liability businesses of the BOC; full-scope on-site examinations on the BCom.

Small- and medium-sized commercial banks: on-site examinations on internal controls of the CITIC bank, large credit risks of the CEB, credit asset quality of China Guangfa Bank, capital management of China Zheshang Bank, corporate governance of the Bank of Jiangsu and off-balance-sheet business of the

Nanchong City Commercial Bank.

Policy banks, the CDB, the PSBC and financial asset management companies: on-site examinations on overseas credit asset and loans to real estate industry and industries with overcapacities of the CDB, overseas credit asset of the EIBC, remediation and three types of loans of the ADBC, remediation, interbank business and off-balance-sheet business of the PSBC, and commercial businesses of the COAMC.

Small- and medium-sized rural financial institutions: on-site examinations by the CBRC head office on performance of one provincial credit cooperative association, overall risk management and compliance of one rural commercial bank, and compliance of two village and township banks; the CBRC organized 31 provincial offices (Beijing, Shanghai, Tibet, Ningbo and Shenzhen offices were not included) to carry out on-site examinations on internal control effectiveness and asset quality of rural cooperative financial institutions.

Foreign banks: coordination on-site examinations on interest rate risk on banking book, which was the first system-wide coordinated examination on foreign banks, covering Heng Seng Bank (China), Shinhan Bank (China) and China CITIC Bank International.

Non-bank financial institutions: on-site examinations on trust companies including CITIC Trust Co., Ltd. and Yingda International Trust Co., Ltd.; on-site examinations on Sinopec Finance Co., Ltd., China Huangneng Co., Ltd. and CITIC Finance Co., Ltd.; Nine on-site examination items on financial leasing companies including ICBC Financial Leasing Co., Ltd., CCB Financial Leasing Co., Ltd., ICBC Financial Leasing Co., Ltd.; on site examination on Chery Motor Finance Service Co., Ltd. and full-scope on-site examinations on Fortune Auto Finance Co., Ltd. and Sichuan Jincheng Consumer Finance Limited Company.

4.Risk resolution and market exit

(1)Strengthening risk resolution and actively disposing risks. First, the CBRC improved risk resolution regulations, actively adopted reorganizing measures to protect bank funds. Second, the CBRC urged banking institutions to conduct five-category loan classification and risk checks, and prepare contingency plans for risks. Third, the CBRC adopted market approaches and "one project, one measure" principle in disposing trust risks. Fourth, the CBRC developed "Communication Platform of Financial Risk Resolution for Enterprise Groups" for the CBRC internal departments and local offices to learn and exchange best practices in disposing risks. Fifth, the CBRC participated in discussions about "Recovery and Resolution Plan" with international supervisory authorities to fully understand the general risks of multinational banks and supervisory focuses in other countries and advance consensus and cooperation with supervisory authorities of home and host countries.

(2)Introducing private capital and emphasizing resolution of existing risks. The CBRC issued the *Notice on Encouraging and Guiding Private Capital to Participate in the Ownership Reform of Rural Credit Cooperatives* to actively support private capital to participate in property right reforms and M&A of rural credit cooperatives.

◎ Reorganization of the Hainan Bank achieved significant progress

In 2014, the CBRC actively promoted the clean-up of Jin Pai Urban Credit Cooperative in Lingao, Hainan province, and reorganized it into the Hainan Bank, which marked the clean-up of the last urban credit cooperative nationwide. The Jin Pai Urban Credit Cooperative was founded in July, 1993, and became insolvent in 2002 when the Guangdong branch of the PBC decided to conduct the clean-up. In recent years, the CBRC worked with the local government and the PBC in handling historical problems of the cooperative, and introduced investors to purchase debt and reorganize it into a municipal commercial bank. On January 23, 2015, the CBRC approved the establishment of the Hainan Bank based on the Jin Pai Urban Credit Cooperative.

5.Supervisory penalties and punishment

In 2014, through various kinds of on-site examinations, the CBRC identified a total of RMB5.1 trillion funds that were involved in regulation violation, penalized 2,157 banking financial institutions, and disqualified 22 senior executives. Administrative penalties were imposed in cases of non-compliance of banking financial institutions and bank staff's breaches of internal policies.

III. Supervisory cooperation and coordination

1.Domestic supervisory cooperation and information sharing

In 2014, the CBRC continued intensifying cooperation and coordination with relevant government agencies, local governments and other financial regulatory authorities. The CBRC worked with the NDRC, the Ministry of Finance, the PBC and the National Auditing Administration to step up regulation of local government debt and standardize financing mechanism for local governments to borrow money. The CBRC worked with the Ministry of Finance and the China Securities Regulatory Commission (CSRC) to establish and improve mechanisms regarding regulation on trust insurance funds, financing through public listing of trust companies and financial leasing companies, informing of supervision on finance companies, and supervision on financial asset management groups. The CBRC deepened coordination mechanism and held joint meetings with the PBC, the CSRC and the China Insurance Regulatory Commission (CIRC). The CBRC also informed the Ministry of Finance, the PBC and relevant government agencies of problems and risks found in examinations on banking institutions to strengthen supervisory coordination.

2.Cross-border supervisory cooperation

(1)Cross-border supervisory cooperation. In 2014, the CBRC signed MOUs on bilateral supervisory cooperation with the Bank of Ghana, Swedish Financial Supervisory Authority, the Bank of Mongolia, Peru's Superintendency of Banking and Insurance and Qatar Central Bank, and the *Exchange of Letters of Bilateral Supervisory Cooperation on Overseas Financial Management of Commercial Banks on Behalf of Clients* with French Financial Markets Authority (AMF). By the end of 2014, the CBRC has signed MOUs on bilateral supervisory cooperation or other agreements with its foreign counterparts from 60 countries and regions.

(2)Cross-border supervisory consultations. In 2014, the CBRC held bilateral talks with supervisory authorities from the United States, Taiwan and Hong Kong SAR. In addition, the CBRC actively participated in high-level bilateral and multilateral meetings including the Economic Dialogue of the 6th Round of China-U.S. Strategic and Economic Dialogues, the 6th China-UK Economic and Financial Dialogue, the 2nd China-France High-level Economic and Financial Dialogue, the 2nd China-Swiss Financial Dialogue, the 9th China-EU Financial Dialogue, the 5th Meeting of the China-Brazil Economic and Financial Subcommittee, the 15th Meeting of the China-Russia Financial Cooperation Subcommittee and the 9th Meeting of the China-Kazakhstan Financial Cooperation Subcommittee. The CBRC set up a cross-departmental work group to hold discussions with supervisory authorities of respective countries and implement results of high-level dialogues. On the one hand, these dialogue mechanisms facilitated eligible Chinese banks to set up branches in key countries and helped remove operation restrictions on these banks in some countries. On the other hand, China also made active commitment of further opening up its banking sector.

(3)Coordination with the host regulatory authorities for overseas Chinese banks. In 2014, the CBRC signed the agreement on division of supervision with UK Prudential Regulation Authority to promote Chinese banks in opening up branches in Britain, held Core Supervisory College for ICBC and BOC to strengthen information sharing and supervisory communication with counterparties in key host countries. The CBRC also intensified communication with counterparts in the United States, Chile, Mexico, Luxemburg, Qatar, and Vietnam among others in host countries on risk of and supervision on overseas operations of Chinese banks.

(4)Communication and coordination with regulatory authorities in home jurisdictions of foreign banks in China. In 2014, the CBRC carried out regular working level talks with Hong Kong Monetary Authority (HKMA), Financial Supervisory Service (FSS) of the Republic of Korea, etc.. The CBRC coordinated with nine foreign counterparts from the United States, Australia, Austria, etc. to conduct cross-border on-site examinations on 18 foreign banks in China. The CBRC worked with five counterparts from Hong Kong, Singapore, etc. to carry out eligibility examinations on senior executives. The CBRC also sent staff to attend international supervisory colleges of nearly 20 multinational banks including the HSBC, the DBS, the UBS and the Bank of India.

(5)Active participation in the international financial reform. As a member of the Financial Stability Board (FSB) and the BCBS, the CBRC attended plenary meetings, task forces and research programs, and participated in the agenda design, standard-setting and implementation assessment of the international financial reform, so as to actively perform its international responsibility, learn best practices and improve the prudential regulatory framework of China's banking sector.

Thematic Column 4　　The 18th ICBS held in Tianjin

From September. 22 to 25, 2014, the 18th International Conference of Banking Supervisors (ICBS) was held in Tianjin. ICBS was initiated by the BCBS, and is the largest and most important international conference for banking supervisors worldwide. Held every two years, ICBS have had 17 sessions since 1979, and it is the first time for it to be held in China.

Two hundred and fifty delegates from 110 regulatory authorities in 93 countries and regions participated in the conference, and the plenum and the joint meeting of the BCBS, six meetings on regional supervision, two seminars and six penal discussions were also held in the meantime. During the conference, Premier Li Keqiang received Stefan Ingves, Chairman of the BCBS, and heads of financial regulatory authorities from a number of countries. Vice Premier Ma Kai attended the conference and delivered a keynote speech.

This conference has taken two important themes. One is the "post-Basel III reform agenda" proposed by the BCBS, and another is "finance promotes economic growth" put forward by the CBRC. In the conference, many major issues concerning current international banking regulation reform were discussed, including how the financial system promotes economic growth, how regulatory standards reach balance among simplicity, comparativeness and risk-sensitiveness, the relationship between macro- and micro-prudential regulation and their challenges, the consistency in calculating risk-weighted assets, handling of exposure to sovereignty risks, influence of regulatory reform on long-term financing, the relationship between irregular monetary policies and banking regulations, regulatory standards for non-internationally active banks, etc.. The CBRC also discussed with counterparts from the United States, Germany, the Czech Republic, etc. to strengthen communication and cooperation of bilateral regulation. Senior executives from the BOC and the ICBC, two global systemically important banks, delivered keynote speeches.

The conference demonstrated the progress made in China's banking sector and banking regulation to delegates from banking regulatory authorities worldwide, and deepened communication and understanding between the CBRC and its foreign counterparts.

IV. Organizational development

1.Party mass line education activities

According to the arrangement from the CPC Central Committee, the CBRC followed the general principle of "watching from the mirror, grooming oneself, taking a bath and seeking remedies", focused on eliminating formalism, bureaucracy, hedonism, and extravagance, and developed diligent working style. Built on the results and experience of the first batch of education activities, the CBRC, from February 2014 to October 2014, carried out the second round in party commissions of all the 306 field offices, 1,730 supervisory offices at county/district-level and branches under prefecture-level of financial institutions supervised by the CBRC. By following the instructions of the CPC Central Committee, the CBRC made arrangement for three links of education and opinion hearing, investigating problems and conducting criticism, and correcting mistakes and formulating regulations, and held onto high standards and strict requirement during the process. With concerted efforts, the second round of activities delivered tangible results to the public, and reached goals.

(1)Party members and cadres received compressive mass line education that improved their theoretical understanding and belief.

(2)A number of issues about formalism, bureaucracy, hedonism and extravagance of great public concern were solved, which refreshed the work style throughout the CBRC system. The participants of the second round cut down the number of meetings by 21 percent year-on-year, the number of documents by 13 percent, public expenditure by 27.5 percent and reduced 11 temporary overseas official visit.

(3)The CBRC advanced supervision, and promoted to solve a

Assistant Chairman YANG Jiacai conducted a field trip in Tibet on county-level financial service.

number of issues concerning public interest and "the last kilometer" issues in serving the public. The cut-down ratio of administrative approval items met the requirement.

(4)The CBRC advanced the practice of strict self-discipline by the party, and improved party activities. The results of the education campaign were widely recognized. The 12th central inspection team randomly selected 10 CBRC provincial offices and one financial institution supervised by the CBRC to evaluate the campaign. Among the 337 representatives in the evaluation, 335 rated the campaign and the resolution of issues concerning formalism, bureaucracy, hedonism and extravagance as "good", accounting for 99.4 percent. "Good" and "Fairly good" made up for 100 percent altogether.

2.Anti-corruption initiatives and disciplinary oversight

In 2014, following the anti-corruption strategy formulated by the CPC Central Committee and the State Council, the CBRC centered around the "three changes" and fully implemented the "two responsibilities" by consolidating the professional ethics of leaders, putting on-going efforts into inspections, interviews, administrative oversight, internal audit and handling of complaints and cases, and attaching great importance to capacity building of discipline inspection teams.

(1)Promotion of professional ethics. Party committees of the CBRC at all levels implemented the CPC Central Politburo's "Eight Provisions" and the detailed implementation rules of the CBRC Party Committee as the rigid constraints. The CBRC kept field trips and overseas visits plain, cleaned up and standardized use of offices and official vehicles, kept meetings and notices short, focused on effectiveness and aimed at eliminating formalism, bureaucracy, hedonism and extravagance.

(2)The system for punishing and preventing corruption. The CBRC designed the *2013-2017 Work Plan for Establishing and Improving the System of Punishing and Preventing Corruption*, and made arrangements in five aspects including advancing the anti-corruption system, holding onto developing sound work style, keeping high pressure on corruption and strengthening the leadership of the party. The CBRC also established and improved the financial supervisory coordination mechanism involving the PBC, the CSRC and the CIRC, built up internal control mechanism, and improved the professionalism and independence of supervisory departments including the board of supervisors, inspection, internal audit, compliance and monitoring.

(3)Intensified supervision. The CBRC stepped up and improved inspection, guided CBRC provincial offices and financial institutions supervised by the CBRC head office to summarize experience from inspection, insisted on handling early warnings and minor cases and dealing with general problems with leaders by warning, talks, letters, etc.. The CBRC regularly met and talked with secretaries of discipline inspection commissions in its provincial offices and financial institutions supervised by the CBRC head office. The CBRC diligently prevented and control corruption risks and focus on developing appropriate risk management procedure.

(4)Capacity building of discipline inspection teams. The CBRC followed the principle of "to work with iron, one must be tough" by implementing the "Eight Provisions", rejecting formalism, bureaucracy, hedonism and extravagance, and emphasizing self-discipline. The CBRC set up three talent pools for inspection, audit and case handling respectively, and promoted "three changes" campaign to build up capacity of inspection and produce sound results.

3.Culture building

The CBRC improved social life of the staff and enrich their lives. The CBRC standardized entertainment and sports activities in grass-root offices by specifying the principle of staff-oriented, wide participation, local conditions and thrifty. The CBRC also conducted census of entertainment and sports talents to develop a talent pool for them to play a leading role. The CBRC sent entertainment and sports facilities to grass-root offices, earmarked fund for model families to staff and grass-root offices in areas with harsh conditions for them to purchase facilities, and pair offices for mutual help. The CBRC developed learning mechanisms such as seminars and online classroom for young staff, carried out face-to-face talks between leaders and young staff, and improved bulletin, E-station, weibo, We Chat and other information sharing platforms and information management systems to carry out various activities for them.

Box 20   Socialist core value education campaign

The CBRC strengthened "three guidance". (1) Ideological guidance. The CBRC carried out activities for staff to learn the history of the party, the country and the socialism development, organized staff to watch educational movies including "Immortal Jiao Yulu", "Jiao Yulu" and "Jumei in the Heaven" and party knowledge questionnaire, movie reviews, etc., to lead party members and cadres to learn and advocate the spirit of Jiao Yulu and strengthen the awareness of dedication. (2) Model guidance. The CBRC carried out elections of individual models and departments/offices for outstanding work and practicing the socialist core value. (3) Practice guidance. The CBRC organized young staff to do field trips to grass-root offices, promoted mentorship and book recommendation activities to guide young staff to learn from grassroots and practice.

Box 21　Organizational work of provincial Youth League Work Committees made all-round breakthroughs

According to the principle of "conducting pilot programs first to gain experience for wider application", the CBRC selected five provinces of Zhejiang, Guangdong, Ningxia, Heilongjiang and Hunan respectively from the eastern, southern, western, northern and central China as well as Qingdao to carry out pilot programs of setting up provincial Youth League Work Committees and gave guidance. The six committees cover major banks, securities and insurance institutions in the region, which are highly representative and effective in advancing work on youth workers in the financial industry.

◎ The CBRC Ningxia Office carried out "Changing Work Style and Focusing on Development" campaign

To resolve the problems of inaction or slow responses in supervisory work, the CBRC Ningxia Office launched the campaign of "Changing Work Style and Focusing on Development", which identified Eight Priorities of the supervisory work. In line with the spirit of Party mass line education activities, the campaign focused on solving the problem of "formalism, bureaucracy, hedonism, extravagance". Guided by the anti-corruption strategy , the Ningxia Office strictly implemented "Eight Provisions" and "Two Responsibilities" to strengthen disciplinary inspection and education. By the end of 2014, the priorities set at year beginning had all been completed. The three public consumptions, namely public expenditures for overseas business trips, car purchase and maintenance, and receptions declined by 11 percent year-on-year, meetings declined by 8 percent year-on-year, and files declined by 11 percent year-on-year.

◎ The CBRC Beijing Office publicly released anti-graft hot lines for whistleblowers

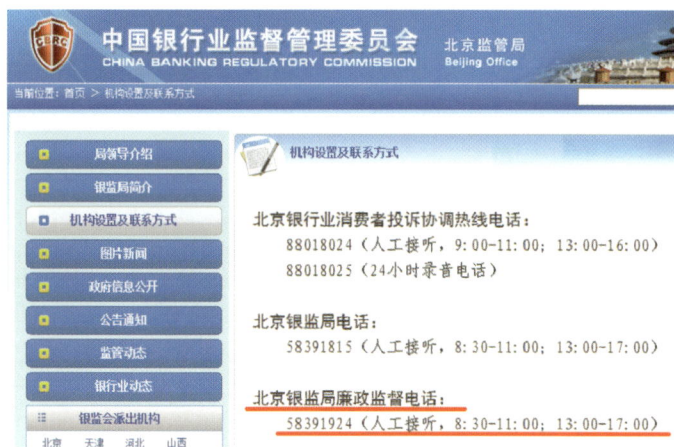

◎ The 2nd Star worker campaign and "Golden Idea" innovation competition

To implement the "innovation-driven growth" strategy and encourage young staff to innovate and improve efficiency, the CBRC took the lead in organizing central financial institutions to carry out the 2014 "Star Worker" campaign. The competition took the form of "Golden Idea" competition that was aimed at innovating products, improving service and raising efficiency so that improved professionalism and service of young staff can promote the awareness and level of service among the whole sector. Financial institutions responded by putting forward a large number of effective innovation plans, and a number of outstanding individuals on common posts emerged. Through WeChat, the voting of "Top Ten Individuals in Work" and "Top Ten Individuals in Service" received 1.18 million votes, and demonstration videos of young workers received 8 million clicks, which effectively spread the "positive energy" of diligent young workers in the financial industry.

◎ Care for staff as a home for staff

In 2014, labor unions of the CBRC stepped up efforts by helping 217 staff in need with RMB 732,600 allocated, donating entertainment and sports facilities worth of RMB 200,000 to local offices in minority areas and areas with harsh conditions, earmarking RMB 50,000 for working groups in Xinjiang province, and applying to Mutual Assistance Center for Staff with Major Diseases for approximately RMB 130,000 for female staff with special diseases.

4.Human resources

As of the end of 2014, the CBRC and its local offices had a total of 23,750 staffs, including 586 at the head office, 5,773 at provincial offices, 13,305 at field offices and 4,086 at supervisory offices at the county level, accounting respectively for 2.47 percent, 24.31 percent, 56.02 percent and 17.20 percent of the total. Of all, female staff numbered 8,332 or 35.08 percent, staff holding undergraduate or higher degrees numbered 19,291 or 81.23 percent of the total, and staff under the age of 45 numbered 12,240 or 51.54 percent.

5.Training

In 2014, the CBRC organized a total of 10 training courses for directors-general and director level officials, training more than 1,200 participants. Through the courses, participants gained insights into major banking supervisory strategies, comprehensively deepened banking reform and promoting supervision by law, effectively combined party spirit and capacity building, strengthened combination of theoretical studies and problem-solving skills, enhanced theoretical foundation, understanding of party policies and strategic thinking, and broadened horizon. The CBRC held the Economic and Financial Elite Seminar for Hong Kong Banking Practitioners that trained 73 senior executives such as chairmen of board and CEOs of large international banks and local banks, which built up their confidence and resolution of joining in the mainland economic development and realizing "Chinese Dream". The CBRC offered trainings especially on on-site examinations, liquidity risk supervision, provision for impairment and internal controls, which effectively improved supervisory staffs' capacity of on-site analysis. The CBRC also helped advance capacity building for financial institutions to manage and respond to risks. In 2014, the CBRC held 22 training programs, amounting to 85 days covering 2,463 practitioners.

6.E-government

The CBRC implemented the philosophy of technology serving supervision and followed the general objective of "unified planning, mechanism improvement, resource sharing and supervision effectiveness improvement" in carrying out informationization of the whole system. The CBRC improved independent research and development capacity and project management capacity, met the supervision needs by developing more than 20 key information systems independently, including EAST and office automation system. EAST, registered for copyright, was used in the CBRC system and proved

Chairman SHANG Fulin, Vice Chairman GUO Ligen and Assistant Chairman YANG Jiacai met participants of the 2014 Economic and Financial Elite Seminar for Hong Kong Banking Practitioners.

to be effective in using big data to improve supervision effectiveness; it was awarded as the "2014 Top Ten Financial Informationization Project". Following the informationization trend and supervision development trend, the CBRC upgraded network and applications infrastructure, and consolidated resources to improve the system capacity and resource efficiency. The CBRC is also gradually using mature, safe and controllable devices to replace old ones to improve system security.

7.Allocation of financial resources

In 2014, with heavier supervisory tasks and tightened budgets, the CBRC strictly practiced economy and allocated its financial resources appropriately so as to maximize the benefit and ensure that banking supervision was carried out smoothly. Reception expenses were strictly controlled, general expenses on meetings and trips were cut down, and offices and official vehicles were cleaned up so as to reduce overhead. Financial resources were prioritized for urgent funding needs. Expenses for supervisory work, including on-site examinations, anti-illegal fundraising and supervisory information system development, etc., accounted for 47 percent of the annual budget, in a bid to improve supervisory efficiency. The need from offices located in remote areas, or those with restoration after natural disasters or heavy tasks of maintaining stability was prioritized.

Photograph by the CBRC staff

Part Five

Prudential Regulation

- Macro-prudential regulation
- Corporate governance and internal controls
- Capital regulation
- Credit risk supervision
- Liquidity risk supervision
- Operational risk supervision
- IT risk supervision
- Market risk supervision
- Country risk supervision
- Reputational risk supervision

I. Macro-prudential regulation

In 2014, while carefully studying the economic and financial developments, the CBRC enhanced its risk monitoring and analysis, and improved the macro-prudential policy framework of the banking sector to guard against systemic risks and risk contagion. It also launched campaigns to increase public awareness on anti-illegal fund raising, guided and facilitated the healthy development of financing guarantee business, and improved relevant policies and regulations, thereby rendering support for sound economic and social development.

1. Strengthening the analysis and monitoring of systemic risks

The CBRC kept monitoring macro-economic situations as well as the developments in key industries and financial markets, and analyzed the impacts of those changes on the banking sector. The off-site surveillance information system was leveraged to collect information in relation to the assets and liabilities, credit risk, market risk, liquidity risk and capital adequacy ratio of the banking institutions, with a view to better analyzing risks of the banking sector. The M_2 to GDP ratio was studied on a quarterly basis in order to continuously monitor and analyze systemic risks. Both bottom-up and top-down stress tests were conducted to analyze the potential risks and assess the risk resilience of both individual banks and the banking system as a whole. The *Guidelines on Stress Testing of Commercial Banks* promulgated in 2007 was further revised, thus improving the policy framework for stress testing. The risk warning system of banking institutions was further strengthened, so as to continuously track the risk profiles of banking institutions and credit risks of bank clients.

2. Advancing the policy-making of macro-prudential supervision

The CBRC worked with relevant ministries in developing the *Guidelines on Systemic Importance Assessment, Capital Requirements and Resolution of Commercial Banks (Provisional),* and the *Guidelines on Implementation of the Counter-cyclical Capital Requirements of Commercial Banks (Provisional),* which further improved the macro-prudential regulatory framework, enhanced the supervision over systemically important banks and explored ways to optimize counter-cyclical supervisory mechanism.

3. Continuously strengthening supervision over systemically important banks

The CBRC urged banking institutions including large banks to improve their corporate governance and risk management, and upgrade their operational and management capacity. In compliance with CBRC's requirement on G-SIFIs, Bank of China (BOC), Industrial and Commercial Bank of China (ICBC) and Agriculture Bank of China (ABC) formulated their respective recovery and resolution plans (RRPs) and further improved their corporate governance. In 2014, the CBRC issued the *Guidelines on Disclosing Assessment Indicators of Global Systemic Importance of Commercial Banks* to enhance market discipline and standardize disclosure of assessment indicators for the global systemically important commercial banks. The *Guidelines on Consolidated Banking Supervision (Provisional)* was revised to further strengthen the consolidated management of banks in response to the new developments and changes in cross-border operations of banks under the new circumstances.

4. Preventing social and financial risks from transmitting into the banking system

Against the backdrop of China's economy adjusting to a new normal of slower growth with continued economic restructuring , the CBRC endeavored to prevent the accumulation and transmission of various latent risks into the banking system. Progress was made in handling illegal fund raising activities, enhancing the investigation and crackdown of such activities, and strengthening risk monitoring and early warning. The CBRC also launched public campaigns to ward off such risks from spreading into the banking sector, thus defending the bottom line of no occurrence of systemic or regional risks. Furthermore, the CBRC assigned local offices to conduct a comprehensive review of the risk profiles of local financing guarantee companies engaged in private funding guarantees, timely resolved relevant risks according to laws and regulations, guided and urged local offices to clean up and standardize non-financing guarantee companies. It also urged banking institutions to standardize the management of financing guarantee loans.

Box 22   Issuing *Guidelines on Disclosing Assessment Indicators of Global Systemic Importance of Commercial Banks*

In November 2011, the Basel Committee on Banking Supervision (BCBS) issued the rules text *Global systemically important banks: assessment methodology and the additional loss absorbency requirement,* which proposed the assessment methodology of global systemically important banks (G-SIBs) that comprises both qualitative and quantitative approaches and encompasses 12 indicators from 5 broad dimensions, including size, cross-jurisdictional activity, interconnectedness, substitutability and complexity. It also required relevant banks to disclose the assessment indicators for their global systemic importance. According to the rules text, the BCBS organizes national regulators to conduct periodic review each year to update the list of global systemically important banks (G-SIBs). An updated version of this document, namely, *Global systemically important banks: updated assessment methodology and the higher loss absorbency requirement* was published in July 2013 that further specified the requirements for disclosure.

In line with the BCBS requirements and the banking reality in China, and by drawing practices from international counterparts, the CBRC issued the *Guidelines on Disclosing Assessment Indicators of Global Systemic Importance of Commercial Banks* in January 2014, specifying the application scope, content, timeframe and ways of information disclosure in this regard.

According to the *Guidelines on Disclosing Assessment Indicators of Global Systemic Importance of Commercial Banks,* commercial banks with an adjusted on- and off-balance sheet asset balance of over RMB1.6 trillion or designated as G-SIBs at the preceding year-end (hereinafter referred to as banks required for information disclosure) are required to disclose information in relation to assessment indicators for global systemic importance. 12 indicators are required to be disclosed, including adjusted on- and off-balance sheet asset balance, intra-financial system assets, intra-financial system liabilities, securities outstanding and other financing vehicles, payments activity, assets under custody, values of underwritten transactions in the security market, OTC derivatives notional value, trading or available-for-sale securities, level 3 assets, cross-jurisdictional claims, and cross-jurisdictional liabilities. Those banks should, in principle, disclose the above required information on their websites or in their annual reports within four months after end of the current accounting year and no later than July 31.

II. Corporate governance and internal controls

1. Enhancing policy framework

In September, the CBRC issued the *Guidelines on Internal Controls of Commercial Banks*, further promoting commercial banks to standardize their internal management and enhance internal controls.

2. Improving the functions of board of directors and board of supervisors

Regulatory policies were effectively communicated and conveyed through observing board meetings and shareholders meetings, holding meetings with board of supervisors and shareholders, and supervisory talks. The CBRC urged and guided commercial banks to strengthen performance assessment, to evaluate the performance of directors and senior management, and to improve the performance assessment data pool for directors, supervisors and senior managers of commercial banks, thus effectively enhancing performance appraisal and curbing the appointment or rotation of the unqualified staff. The CBRC highlighted the role of remuneration in corporate governance and risk controls and required the independency of remuneration committee in commercial banks.

3. Enhancing on-site examinations

The CBRC continuously gave attention to the effectiveness of corporate governance and risk controls of commercial banks, improved corporate governance framework and intensified mechanism of checks and balances. Some examinations focused on whether commercial banks' internal controls are proportionate to their business expansion rate, as well as whether their institutional framework, internal controls, credit control and compliance are up to the standard.

Box 23   Issuing the *Guidelines on Internal Controls of Commercial Banks*

In September, the CBRC revised and issued the *Guidelines on Internal Controls of Commercial Banks* (hereinafter referred to as the *Guidelines*). This revised *Guidelines* guided commercial banks to enhance internal controls from the following four aspects:

In assessing internal controls, specific requirements were continuously improved. The *Guidelines* further supplements the requirements for assessing internal controls, and calls commercial banks to set up an assessment mechanism for internal controls. The *Guidelines* specifies the assessment body, frequency, content, procedures, methods and standards, emphasizes the application of assessment results and highlights the institutional arrangements of the assessment mechanism, with a view to facilitating commercial banks to constantly improve the arrangement and function of their internal controls.

In monitoring internal controls, a long-term mechanism was established and improved. The *Guidelines* introduces requirements for both commercial banks and the CBRC in overseeing internal controls. Internally, commercial banks should establish a monitoring and review mechanism covering all their establishments, products and business process and procedures, while externally the CBRC and its local offices should conduct on-going supervision over commercial banks' internal controls through on-site examinations and off-site surveillance, thus bringing out the synergy between internal and external oversights.

In strengthening regulatory discipline, punishment for violations became tougher. The *Guidelines* adds punitive measures against violations. For commercial banks with deficiencies in internal controls, the CBRC and its local offices require corrective measures to be taken within a set timeframe. Failure of timely correction would warrant punitive regulatory measures.

In providing supervisory guidance, the CBRC strictly followed principle-based supervision. The *Guidelines* specifies the in-principle requirements for internal controls in commercial banks' risk management, information control, organizational structure, accounting methods, staff management, new establishments, and business innovations.

III. Capital regulation

In 2014, the CBRC further improved the policy framework for capital regulation, and guided banking institutions to formulate their annual capital plans, to improve risk governance, and to set the target for capital adequacy ratio (CAR) as well as the plans for capital replenishment and risk-weighted asset (RWA) management. A long-term mechanism for capital replenishment was established to supplement capitals from multiple channels, thus lifting banking institutions' capital management level to realize more intensive and sustainable use of their capitals.

1. Implementing the *Capital Rules of Commercial Banks (Provisional)*

Year 2014 marked the second year for the implementation of the *Capital Rules*. Since its implementation, commercial banks spent great efforts in improving their risk controls and capital management, with progress made in the following aspects. First, capital constraint mechanism was improved, as commercial banks generally developed their respective capital plans and comprehensive risk assessment mechanisms. Second, the business model was gradually changing. MSE loans of commercial banks witnessed accelerated growth in general, while capital-intensive businesses began to shrink. Third, infrastructure development was further strengthened, and more efforts were made in developing the information system and economical capital system of commercial banks. Fourth, with the continued improvement in risk measurement techniques, the granularity of risk measurement was considerably refined.

As of end-2014, 828 commercial banks in China realized an average CAR of 13.2% and the Common Equity Tier 1 (CET 1) ratio of 10.8%, up by 0.99 percentage point and 0.61 percentage point respectively compared with year beginning. The majority banks have been compliant with the regulatory requirement for the phase-in period of the *Capital Rules*.

2. Piloting the implementation of advanced approaches of capital calculation

Six banks including ICBC, ABC, BOC, CCB, BCm and China Merchants Bank (CMB) were approved to implement the advanced approaches of capital calculation, while small- and medium-sized commercial banks with sound management and willingness were also encouraged to opt for these approaches. An on-going regulatory reporting system was developed to conduct off-site surveillance over the implementation of these advanced approaches, and the above mentioned six banks have started submitting the regulatory report since 1 July 2014. On-site examinations for the advanced approaches were conducted to review the management of credit risk, market risk, and operational risk, covering such aspects as the internal models, data base, implementation of policy and procedures, and the support of IT system.

3. Innovating capital instruments by commercial banks

In 2014, commercial banks kick-started the issuance of preferred shares. In April, the CBRC and the CSRC jointly issued the ***Guiding Opinions of CBRC and CSRC on Issuing Preferred Shares as Tier 1 Capital by Commercial Banks*** [Yin Jian Fa No.12, 2014]. After that, ICBC, ABC and BOC successively completed their first offerings of preferred shares. The issuance of tier 2 capital bond instruments entered into a stage of normal issuance, with pilots of overseas offerings successfully conducted and investor base further expanded. In 2014, the total value of tier 2 capital bond instruments issued by 42 banks domestically reached RMB356.9 billion, with the issuing banks ranging from large banks and joint-stock banks to city commercial banks and rural commercial banks, etc.. The ancillary accounting and taxation systems for the new-type capital instruments were articulated.

◎ Agricultural Bank of China issued the first onshore preferred stock on domestic capital market

On November 28, 2014, Agricultural Bank of China issued the first deal of preferred shares worth of RMB40 billion on the Shanghai Stock Exchange, marking the completion of the first preferred stock issuance on Chinese onshore capital market.

The ceremony of preferred shares issuance of ABC.

◎ BoCom completed the first deal of offshore Tier 2 capital bond issuance among Chinese banks headquarters

BoCom issued offshore Tier 2 capital bond on December 3rd 2014, the first Chinese bank to finish such deal from its head office. The Tier 2 instrument with loss absorption features is in compliance with Basel III and

CBRC's requirements and is composed by two bond offering tranches: a US$1.2 billion 10NC5 and a EUR500 million 12NC7.

IV. Credit risk supervision

1. Local government financing platform (LGFP) loans

In 2014, following the principle of "total volume control, classified management, differentiated treatment and staged disposal", the CBRC focused on loan volume control, loan structure optimization, risk segregation and responsibility clarification, and steadily pressed ahead with the regulation of LGFP loans, thereby putting the overall risks well under control.

First, strictly controlling the total amount of LGFP loans. Guided by the principle that "credit should be secured for on-going projects, reduced for redundant projects and controlled for new projects", banking institutions were not allowed to scale up the volume of LGFP loans. Approval criteria such as full coverage of borrower's cash flow, proper collaterals and an asset-to-liability ratio not exceeding 80% shall be strictly observed for the extension of new LGFP loans.

Second, continuously optimizing LGFP loan structure. Newly issued loans were channeled to primarily support the reasonable financing needs of qualified provincial financing platforms, low-income housing projects and the key national projects under construction. Loans extensions were gradually cut back to LGFPs with low cash flow coverage, weak local fiscal support, high liability-to-asset ratio and substandard collaterals so as to gradually realize credit exit from such LGFPs.

Third, gradually mitigating risks of loan stock. Banking institutions prudently calculated the cash flow coverage of LGFPs, and adopted a classified management method in setting aside provisions respectively for four categories of LGFP loans based upon the extent of cash flow coverage, including full coverage, largely coverage, half coverage and zero coverage, thus consolidating the risk management foundation. Credit exit, contract revision, repayment correction, collateral supplementation and effective capital injection were specified for LGFP loans. Reforms of existing LGFP loans were pushed forward and risk resilience was enhanced. Banking institutions actively negotiated with LGFPs on debt servicing sources on a case-by-case basis every month, so that near-term risks were effectively contained without major default event occurring.

Fourth, strengthening the comprehensive risk management. The CBRC established a comprehensive statistical system for LGFP debts, covering bank loans, corporate bonds, medium-term notes, short-term financing notes, trust schemes and wealth management products, etc., and strengthened consolidated supervision over both credit and non-credit financing of LGFPs. Banking institutions were required to take into account whether the total scale of the LGFP debts is proportionate to their debt-servicing capacity.

The CBRC continued to strengthen policy communications with Ministry of Finance as well as other ministries, and participated in the promulgation of *Opinions of the State Council on Strengthening the Management of Local Government Debts* [GuoFa, No. 43, 2014] to actively advance the demand-side management of LGFP loans.

◎ **Anhui prevented the occurance of NPLs or default event of LGFP loans**

In conducting supervision on LGFP loans, the CBRC Anhui Office took the following measures, including, 1) conveying regulatory policy in a timely manner with strengthened policy guidance and training; 2) enhancing name-list management strictly, improving the statistical system of full-caliber liabilities and reinforcing the risk warning and information sharing; and 3) studying carefully the current situations and putting forward supervisory opinions. The stock of LGFP loans in Anhui Province has been decreasing for four consecutive years without the occurrence of NPLs or default event.

2. Real estate loans

In 2014, the CBRC continued to enhance off-site surveillance and on-site examinations over credit risks of real estate loans extended by banking institutions, improved data quality for monitoring risks associated with such loans, emphasized the oversight and early warning of both market and credit risks in the regional property sector, and strictly investigated into and penalized any real estate credit extension that violates laws and regulations, thereby defending its bottom line of no occurrence of regional or systemic risks. In the meantime, banking institutions were guided to better support residential housing finance, and encouraged to finance shantytown renovation and low-income housing projects eligible for credit according to the principles of risks controllable and financially viable. Banking institutions were required to support the reasonable loan demands for first-time home buyers and second home buyers whose first home size is below local average with a shortened credit approval cycle. The CBRC continuously guided commercial banks to closely follow the developments of the real estate sector, enhanced data collection and analysis of the market, better identified and understood risks so as to anticipate risk trends and come up with contingency plan in a timely manner.

◎ **The CBRC Hainan Office achieved notable results in preventing the risks of real estate loans**

The prevention of real estate loan risks was a vital task for the CBRC Hainan office as its real estate loan balance accounted for 21.2 percent of the total loans under its jurisdiction. The CBRC Hainan Office conducted on-going monitoring and stress testing, launched inspections into banking institutions with relatively high proportion or high growth rate of newly issued real estate loans, and urged institutions to formulate associated risk contingency plans and implement supervisory requirements as well as the risk management measures. In the context of increasing pressure from the rebound of NPLs, the quality of real estate loans in Hainan did not decline substantially. As of end-2014, the NPL ratio of real estate loans in Hainan province was 0.67 percent, which was 0.35 percentage point lower than the NPL of total loans.

3. Concentration risks

In 2014, the CBRC continued to follow the requirements in supervising concentration risks and actively urged banking institutions to effectively manage such risks. First, concentration risk indicators in the early warning system were revised, and the early warning system of concentration risks was improved. Banking institutions with risk indicators exceeding regulatory limits were urged to make risk mitigation plans within a specified timeframe, so as to fend off risks. Second, concentration risks were prevented along with credit restructuring so as to channel more credit to micro and small enterprises (MSEs), agro-related development, key national projects, strategic emerging industries, as well as foreign trade and Chinese enterprises' "going global" initiative. Banking institutions were encouraged to satisfy households' reasonable demand for home loans while avoiding the pursuit of large-value loans, in particular loans for industries with high pollution, high-energy consumption and overcapacity and for sectors with high risks. Third, supervision over concentration risks of inter-bank businesses was enhanced in that commercial banks' lending exposure to a single financial institution should be strictly controlled, monitored and examined so that any violations shall be punished according to the law.

4. Off-balance sheet risks

In 2014, the CBRC continued to enhance the risk monitoring and examination in wealth management businesses, credit asset transfer, inter-bank financing and payment, and other off-balance sheet activities, and closely monitored the changes of off-balance sheet risk exposure, with a view to guarding against the contagion of such risks.

(1)Facilitating commercial banks to develop a comprehensive consolidated management system. In line with the principle of "substance over form", the CBRC developed an all-round and multi-tiered system for credit classification, capital calculation and provisioning that covers non-credit and off-balance sheet assets.

(2)Further regulating wealth management businesses of commercial banks. Banks were required to follow the principles of independent accounting, risk segregation, conduct regulation and centralized management in pursuing structural reforms for their wealth management business. Dedicated wealth management departments were established by banks to centrally manage that business.

(3)Further improving the supervisory system for off-balance sheet businesses. The CBRC drafted the *Rules on Managing the Off-balance Sheet Business of Commercial Banks,* and *Rules on Managing the Entrusted Loans,* and amended the *Guidelines on Managing Off-balance Sheet Risks of Commercial Banks*.

(4)Intensifying on-site examinations over off-balance sheet businesses. The CBRC conducted on-site examinations and thematic inspections on banks' proprietary business, wealth management business, underwriting business, acceptances, commitments, letters of credit, and letters of guarantee, thus timely preventing and mitigating risks.

Box 24　Non-performing loans (NPLs) of commercial banks

As of end-2014, the NPL balance of China's commercial banks stood at RMB842.6 billion, with an increase of RMB250.6 billion. The NPL ratio was 1.25%, up by 0.25 percentage point compared with year beginning. In terms of regional distribution and sector concentration, NPLs expanded from east coastal areas to central and western regions and were concentrated on manufacturing as well as wholesale and retail sectors. In terms of business scale and customer types, NPLs shifted from MSEs to medium-sized and large enterprises and from corporate clients to private customers. With regards to business nature, NPLs transmitted from off-balance sheet to on-balance sheet businesses.

The banking sector set aside adequate provisions against rising NPLs. As of end-2014, the loan loss provision of commercial banks amounted to RMB1.96 trillion, with a provisioning coverage ratio of 232.1% and provision ratio of 2.9%. With adequate provisions, commercial banks enjoyed strong gone-concern loss absorbing capacity (GLAC).

◎ The CBRC Shandong Office strengthens supervision on cross-regional credit extension of small- and medium-sized banks

To regulate non-prudential activities, the CBRC Shandong office drafted the *Guidelines on Cross-regional Credit Extension of Small- and Medium-sized Banks*, which specifies the definition of cross-regional credit extension, its geographical scope, and regulatory requirements on qualification for conducting cross-regional credit extension, risk control measures and monitoring and filing issues. It also urged small- and medium-sized commercial banks to collaborate with local government and the CBRC field offices in Shandong to establish joint management mechanism on large-volume credit issuance. Currently, 33 small- and medium-sized banks have regulated and sorted out the cross-regional credit extension business.

◎ The CBRC Shanxi Office formulated contingency plan for major and specialized risks

In order to enhance the rationality and responsiveness in coping with various risk events, the CBRC Shanxi Office established a batch of contingency plans, including *Working Mechanism of the CBRC Shanxi Office on Coping with Major Banking Risks, Contingency Plan of the Shanxi Banking Industry on Handling Major Credit Risks, Guiding Opinions of the CBRC Shanxi Office for Properly coping with Major Risk Events of the Banking Industry, Contingency Plan of the CBRC Shanxi Office on Handling Major Institutional Risks, Contingency Plan of the Shanxi Banking Industry on Handling Major Corporate Risks,* and *Contigency Plan on Resolving Bank Run*.

◎ The CBRC Shanghai Office emphasized risk alert in key areas with enhanced control of both NPL balance and ratio

In 2014, the CBRC Shanghai Office improved its capability of risk regulation by enhancing risk alert, identification and resolution. It issued 24 pieces of risk warnings and alerts for steel trade loans, copper trade loans, commercial property loans and credit card businesses, thus sending an early warning to commodity financing risks in copper trade. "Double control" on non-performing loan (NPL) (i.e. control on NPL balance and NPL ratio) has been proceeding in an orderly manner. Risk resolution plans for steel trade have been established. By the end of 2014, NPL ratio of Shanghai banking sector stood at 0.89%, and a total worth of

RMB 39.853 billion bad assets has been disposed of by major commercial banks, with a value of RMB 21.916 billion bad loans resolved in steel trade.

V. Liquidity risk supervision

In 2014, based on the overall strategy of full coverage and dynamic supervision, the CBRC made continued efforts to improve the liquidity risk prevention framework and urged banking institutions to intensify liquidity risk monitoring and stress testing. Furthermore, the CBRC constantly improved regulatory policies and took various measures to increase the effectiveness of liquidity risk supervision.

The CBRC issued and implemented the *Rules on Liquidity Risk Management of Commercial Banks (Provisional),* which sets out a liquidity risk supervision framework that combines qualitative with quantitative methods, emphasizes micro and macro prudential regulations, and consolidates the supervisory requirements for Chinese and foreign banks. In the meantime, the CBRC enhanced training and guidance for supervisory staff as well as for banks, promoting the effective implementation of regulatory policies.

The CBRC issued the *Notice on Adjusting Loan-to-Deposit Calculation Methods of Commercial Banks,* which promoted banks to enhance liquidity risk management, helped banking institutions further support the real economy, agro-related undertakings, and MSEs, and facilitated the in-depth development of China's financial markets.

In September 2014, the CBRC, Ministry of Finance and the PBC jointly issued the *Notice on Strengthening Deposit Deviation Management of Commercial Banks* [Yin Jian Ban Fa No. 236, 2014], which sets a month-end deposit deviation indicator to contain banks from taking deposits in violation of regulations and inflating their deposit totals. Banking institutions were urged to establish a scientific performance appraisal system, correct the behaviors of month-end deposit absorption to meet the regulatory requirement, and curb manipulated fluctuations in deposit balance, so as to create a sound environment for banks to enhance their liquidity risk management.

The approaches and tools for liquidity risk supervision were improved. In order to intensify liquidity risk analysis and monitoring, the CBRC closely watched the interbank liquidity changes, and organized major commercial banks to conduct liquidity risk stress testing. Through reasonable design of stress tests, the CBRC urged and guided banks to improve their methodologies and the quality of stress tests.

Box 25   Issuing the *Notice on Adjusting Loan-to-Deposit Calculation Methods of Commercial Banks*

In 2014, in response to the increasingly diversified asset-liability structure of China's banking sector, the CBRC further improved the loan-to-deposit (LTD) ratio regulation, and issued the *Notice on Adjusting Loan-to-Deposit Calculation Methods of Commercial Banks* effective from July 1, 2014.

First, the scope of currencies in the calculation of LTD ratio was adjusted. Instead of computing both RMB- and foreign-currency-denominated loans, the revised methods compute only RMB-denominated loans in LTD ratio and make it a formal regulatory indicator, while LTD ratio with loans denominated in both RMB and foreign currencies and separately in foreign currencies will only be used as a monitoring indicator. This adjustment conforms to current laws and regulations as well as requirements set forth in Basel III and *Rules on Liquidity Risk Management of Commercial Banks (Provisional)* on separately managing the liquidity risks of significant currencies. Meanwhile, regulatory arbitrage through currency conversion can be prevented by monitoring the LTD ratio both in foreign and local currencies and separately in foreign currecies.

Second, the numerators of LTD ratio were revised. In addition to the deduction of agro-related re-lending, MSE financial debts, agro-related financial bonds, and farming household and MSE loans issued by township and village bank as the leading bank already in practice, the adjusted calculation further removed three items from the numerators, namely, 1) bonds issued by commercial banks with a remaining maturity of no less than one year and with

no early redemption clauses; 2) MSE loans through re-lending of the central bank; and 3) loans extended by commercial banks with funds of international financial organizations or overseas governments. As the above-mentioned loans enjoy clear and stable funding sources, there is no need for matching deposits.

Third, the denominators were revised as well. The adjusted computation adds two items as elligble deposits: one is the negotiable certificate of deposit (CD) issued by banks to enterprises and individuals; and the second is the net deposits of foreign bank subsidiaries in China from their overseas parent banks with a maturity of over one year. The first category is a stable source of funding for banks. Given a considerable amount of capital of locally incorporated foreign banks comes from their parent banks, the calculation of net capital with over one year maturity as deposits will help foreign banks fully utilize this stable source of funding to expand their business and support the real economy in China.

Media perspective 5   More flexible LTD ratio for credit loosening

Since 1990s, the LTD ratio was introduced by PBC for certain banks, and was incorporated into the *Law on Commercial Banks*. After the establishment of the CBRC, *Law on Commercial Banks* was revised once, but LTD ratio was not removed. Instead, it has been in effect under the oversight of the CBRC until now.

In June 2014, the CBRC issued the *Notice on Adjusting Loan-to-Deposit Calculation Methods of Commercial Banks*, which adjusted the calculation methods of LTD ratio. Six items including MSE and agro-related loans were deducted from loan computation, while two more items like negotiable CD and foreign banks' net capital with over one year maturity from overseas parent banks were added in deposit computation so that commercial banks can release more credit resources for the real economy.

This regulatory flexibility is a blessing for banks that border on regulatory threshold. By September 2014, the LTD ratio of CCB, BOC and BOCom stood at 72.02 percent, 71.65 percent, and 73.92 percent respectively, all approaching the regulatory ceiling of 75 percent.

The LTD calculation adjustment can release more capital to support the real economy and benefit enterprises as well. As estimated by GUAN Qingyou, "If inter-bank deposits can be computed as general deposits, it will release 7.4 trillion more funds."

(Source: Economic Daily, by Chen Guojing)

Box 26   Issuing the *Rules on Liquidity Risk Management of Commercial Banks*

In order to promote the liquidity risk management and thus maintain the sound operation of banking system, the CBRC promulgated the *Rules on Liquidity Risk*

Management of Commercial Banks (Provisional) based on international regulatory standards, China's liquidity risk management practices as well as public opinions solicited. The **Rules** will help to refine and upgrade liquidity risk management of commercial banks, better balance asset and liability structure, and enhance liquidity risk resilience of commercial banks and the banking system as a whole.

First, qualitative regulatory requirement was combined with quantitative one. The CBRC consolidated the qualitative and quantitative regulatory requirements for liquidity risk supervision prescribed in different laws and regulations, and enriched the qualitative requirements. It further sorted out the liquidity risk indicators by introducing the liquidity coverage ratio of Basel III, and distinguished between indicators of regulatory compliance and monitoring indicators.

Second, micro- and macro-prudential perspectives were combined. While intensifying liquidity risk management and supervision of individual institutions, regulators and commercial banks are also required to closely watch and study the impact of macro-economic and financial policy changes as well as financial market developments on banks' liquidities. Through monitoring and studying the liquidity of the overall market and considering the major market headwinds in stress testing, the CBRC was able to identify any sign of liquidity stress and funding cost hike and take responsive measures in a timely manner.

Third, the regulatory requirements for Chinese and foreign banks were unified. The **Rules** unified the common regulatory requirements for Chinese and foreign banks in liquidity risk management, so as to build a complete framework for Chinese and foreign banks to manage and supervise liquidity risks. Specific requirements were made in consideration of the characteristics of foreign banks in liquidity risk management.

◎ **The CBRC Jiangsu office set up liquidity mutual assistance contingency mechanism of rural cooperative institutions**

Under the guidance of the CBRC Jiangsu office, Jiangsu rural credit union established a liquidity mutual assistance mechanism to ease liquidity stress resulted from concentrated deposit withdrawal or bank run. The mutual assistance mechanism should be market-oriented with lending rate benchmarking against spot interbank rates. When large-scale deposit withdrawal subdues or the mutual assistance fund expires, the institutions receiving assistance should raise fund timely to repay the principal and interest.

VI.Operational risk supervision

In 2014, the CBRC urged banking institutions to actively guard against operational risks, set appropriate risk appetite and tolerance and improve operational risk management. In conducting targeted examination on operational risks, the CBRC continued to play its role in investigating and monitoring major banking cases.

In accordance with the operational risk requirements set in the **Capital Rules of Commercial Banks (Provisional)**, commercial banks endeavored to: 1) improve the corporate governance, set up basic operational risk management framework, and develop monitoring, review and training mechanism for operational risks; 2) establish operational risk reporting system, promote the monitoring of key risk indicators and application of operational risk loss database, and specify the responsibilities, identification, classification, reporting and review of risk loss incidents; 3) establish a self-assessment system for all function lines, strengthen risk analysis and research, and upgrade the operational risk management level; 4) proactively conduct business impact analysis and business continuity risk review in the respect of business continuity management, and expand the coverage, standardize the process and improve the quality of assessment.

The CBRC adhered to the principle of emphasizing investigation and prevention with prevention as the priority in controlling banking cases. First, policy framework was further improved by issuing the *Notice on Establishing and Improving the "Two Line" Risk Prevention and Control Accountability Mechanism, Notice on Enhancing Credit Control* and *Prohibiting Illegal Credit Extension, Rules on Risk Review for Cases of Banking Institutions,* and *Rules on Punishment Information Management for Banking Professionals*, and by revising *the Statistical System for the Prevention and Control of Banking Cases*. Second, efforts were made in the investigation and monitoring of major cases. It strengthened the investigation and monitoring of typical cases and major risk incidents of different types of banking institutions. It promoted the accountability mechanism for cases, conveyed the requirements for case prevention, and regularly analyzed and notified the features of cases, and intensified risk alerts in key business areas, and urged institutions with cases occurred to enhance internal controls and risk management. Third, on-site examination was strengthened. The CBRC headquarters and its local offices organized comprehensive examinations on the security of automatic telling machines (ATMs) and automatic banking services of the supervised banking institutions.

◎ The CBRC developed anti–fraud information management system of the banking industry

In 2014, the CBRC promoted research endeavor on the prevention and control of banking fraud. Building upon systematic analysis and research on banking anti-fraud efforts both at home and abroad, it put forward policy recommendations on establishing anti-fraud working mechanism to monitor, identify, review and resolve risks. To facilitate anti-fraud information sharing, it developed the anti-fraud information management system of the banking industry, which collects and consolidates the banking fraudulent information, realizes electronic reporting, analysis and distribution of the information, so that information sharing was further enhanced and support could be given to prevent fraud at various links of the business flow.

◎ The CBRC Jiangxi Office launched the campaign of the Year of Conduct Rectification against Banking Cases 2014

In 2014, in order to enhance compliance culture and prevent andcontrol banking cases, the CBRC Jiangxi Office formalized thematic examination on banking cases control for the senior executives.During the year, 10 percent of the banking senior executives in Jiangxi were randomly selected to sit the exams of banking cases prevention, so that the compliance culture can be further enhanced in a top-down manner. The effect was revealing, as both the number and value of banking cases declined, with a fall of 75 percent in banking cases occurred and a fall of 43.75 percent in the value exposed form a year earlier.

◎ The CBRC Ningbo Office took series of measures to strengthen the conduct supervision of banking employees

First, the CBRC Ningbo Office developed a management system for local banking employees, which centralized the information flow, rule-breaking activities and compliance status of the banking employees so that transparency was enhanced. Second, it promoted the policy of "conduct due diligence before hiring and sign endorsement before resignation" to urge banks to check on the inflow and outflow of employees strictly. Third, it guided the local banking association to formulate self-discipline convention on banking employees, to organize compliance exams for those having serious irregularity activities and put a restriction on the executives failing the exams from taking office.

VII. IT risk supervision

1. Improving supervisory mechanism

In September, the CBRC, NDRC, Ministry of Information and Technology jointly issued the **Guiding Opinions on Strengthening the Banking Cyber Security and Information Technology Construction through the Application of Secure and Controllable Information Technologies** [Yin Jian Fa, No. 39, 2014]. The CBRC also compiled the **Annual Report on Information Technologies of the Banking Sector in 2013**. Regulatory policies regarding off-site and centralized IT outsourcing were drafted with assessment details specified. Furthermore, it conducted research on classifying regulatory policies against different IT status and risk profiles of various banking institutions.

2. Enhancing supervision

In addition to joint-stock commercial banks and city commercial banks, the IT supervisory rating was further applied to cover large commercial banks, China Development Bank (CDB), Postal Savings Bank of China (PSBC) and rural cooperative financial institutions, and the respective ratings were incorporated into the institutional rating system. On-site examinations were organized in the areas of online banking and e-banking. The CBRC kept tracking and monitoring sector and systemic risks, and developed a working mechanism to discuss and address cyber security risks of major commercial banks. Besides, banks' business continuity was further strengthened and banks' emergency response to operational events was enhanced. The reporting system for off-site IT surveillance of banking institutions was upgraded and guidelines for reporting were specified. The CBRC issued the **Regulatory Data Standards of the CBRC (SMEs and Rural Financial Institutions)** (version 2.0), specifying the regulatory standards, further expand the scope of data collection and application review. It helped push banking institutions to analyze and identify the problems existing in its data management and IT system development with regulatory standards as the benchmark, so as to comprehensively improve management expertise.

3. Promoting IT innovations of the banking sector

The CBRC stressed the importance of the banking information technology being secure and controllable. Security review of key information and internet infrastructure of the banking sector was conducted, strategic alliance for secure and controllable information technology innovation of the banking sector was established, and technology laboratories were built to centralize the endeavor of providing solutions and promoting technological innovations.

Box 27   Preventing and mitigating IT outsourcing risks of the banking sector

In 2014, a united supervisory platform for IT outsourcing of the banking sector was built by the CBRC to consolidate banking resources in order to monitor systemic risks arising from outsourcing. 130 banking institutions were organized to conduct joint on-site examinations on over 26 highly concentrated key outsourcing vendors. Through two months' examinations, a large amount of sectoral and fundamental problems were identified, and highly problematic outsourcing vendors and key risks were centrally treated and handled, thus mitigating sector risks. Risk supervision and management was further emphasized for pronounced problems in off-site and centralized outsourcing of the banking sector, with

the *Notice on Strengthening Management of Off-Site and Centralized IT Outsourcing Risks in Banking Institutions* and *Notice on Conducting Assessment for Off-Site and Centralized IT Outsourcing Risks in Banking Institutions* successively promulgated. Outsourcing vendors are not required but can volunteer to apply for regulatory assessment so that such outsourcing services can be incorporated into supervisory assessment. The CBRC conducted risk monitoring, on-site assessment and risk disposal on a regular basis and fended off systemic risks associated with outsourcing in the banking sector.

VIII. Market risk supervision

In 2014, the CBRC guided banking institutions to further improve market risk management system with enhanced accountability, conduct in-depth market research, improve the risk analysis framework of financial markets, and utilized various measurement tools to study and identify interest rate and foreign exchange rate risks. In response to the interest rate reform and foreign exchange changes, banks were guided to conduct stress tests and make risk supervision better targeted and more forward-looking. The CBRC also called upon banks to set risk limits, and conduct review and examination regularly and periodically so as to better manage market risks. By combining targeted examinations with thematic research, the CBRC also organized banks to conduct targeted examinations over interest rate risks of the banking book.

IX. Country risk supervision

In 2014, the CBRC continued to monitor banking institutions in enhancing country risk management. First, it urged foreign banks to timely report the external ratings, financial status, significant operational risk changes of their parent banks, major regulatory measures for their parent banks taken by host regulatory authorities, and significant events with major impacts on the parent operations. A dedicated team was called to be established to assess and monitor the operating environment of their head offices by country and region, thus preventing cross-border risk transmission. Second, the CBRC urged large commercial banks to incorporate country risk management into their comprehensive risk management framework, and enhance the identification, measurement, monitoring and control of country risks on a consolidated basis, so as to step up their country risk assessment capabilities. Third, the mechanism for country risk provisioning was continuously enhanced. Fourth, the model of country risk limit was further improved, with relevant rules governing country risk rating and limit specified. Fifth, the country risk stress testing was intensified. Sixth, IT system development was further advanced so as to enhance IT support for country risk management.

X. Reputational risk supervision

In 2014, the CBRC further facilitated the inclusion of reputational risk management into the comprehensive risk management framework, and guided commercial banks to prevent and mitigate various reputational risk events. First, through effective guidance, the CBRC promoted the mitigation of reputational risks. It issued over 120 pieces of risks alerts against rule-breaking activities, banking cases and banking system failures, and facilitated the handling of over 100 pieces of client complaints. It organized 119 pieces of reputational risk reviews and response rehearsals, and conducted 125 training sessions on reputational risk management. Second, it urged commercial banks to intensify reputational risk management and upgrade their reputational risk management mechanism and expertise by utilizing the new media. For banking outlets with frequent incidence of reputational risk events, the focus was to train the head as well as the front-desk staff of such outlets to raise their risk awareness. Third, the CBRC timely monitored and resolved reputational risk events. Leveraging the electronic monitoring platform, commercial banks kept real-time monitoring of the media, and took the initiative to address reputational risk incidents, including customer complaints and banking cases exposed by the media, thus effectively mitigating reputational risk events. Fourth, the CBRC deepened the study into quantitative indicators of reputational risks. It explored ways to build a reputational risk supervisory assessment framework for banking institutions and took regulatory measures accordingly.

Photograph by the CBRC staff

Part Six

Banking Consumer Protection and Education

- Development of regulatory framework
- Promoting banking institutions to fulfill their duties
- Promoting financial literacy
- Strengthening consumer protection survey and research

I. Development of regulatory framework

1. Improving the organizational structure

In February, the CBRC issued the *Guiding Opinions on Supervision of CBRC Local Offices over Consumer Protection*, requiring the CBRC local offices to strengthen the development of the consumer protection function, guiding them to oversee the protection of banking consumers based on the principle of "Prevention First, Education Oriented, Legal Rights Protected and Resolution Coordinated". As of end-2014, 31 provincial offices of the CBRC had set up respective consumer protection departments and another 5 had assigned full-time employees to take charge of consumer protection.

2. Establishing the consumer protection appraisal and evaluation mechanism

In August, the CBRC issued the *Rules for Appraising and Evaluating the Consumer Protection of Banking Institutions (Provisional),* according to which the actual consumer protection performance and effectiveness of banking institutions will be appraised and evaluated in the spirit of soundness, objectivity, fairness, motivation and restriction against the aspects of consumer protection rules and policies development, measures supporting the implementation thereof, effectiveness of consumer protection work, internal appraisal and management, and handling of key issues. The *Rules* aim to guide banking institutions to ensure compliance and self-discipline.

3. Strengthening the consumer risk alert mechanism

In 2014, the CBRC strengthened the efforts to analyze the causes of and countermeasures for financial fraud, security of personal financial information and other topical issues. The CBRC timely made risk alerts to the public and banking institutions through a variety of means, such as producing and broadcasting public service ads jointly with the China National Radio and making risk alert statements on the CBRC website, etc..

4. Improving the consumer complaints handling mechanism

In 2014, the CBRC promoted the use of the banking consumer complaints handling system across the CBRC and its local offices. As a result, the handling, query and analysis of consumer complaints can be dealt with on one single platform. The principle is that the complaints will be handled by banking institutions before they are submitted to the supervisory authorities if they are not resolved, and the complaints will be handled by branch offices before they are submitted to the banks' head office if they are not resolved. For complaints unresolved by banking institutions, the CBRC will accept them and make coordination for the handling.

Box 28   The High-level banking consumer protection steering committee was established

In September, the CBRC issued the **Notice on Establishing the High-Level Banking Consumer Protection Steering Committee,** pursuant to which the high-level steering committee was established. Comprising members from the CDB, large commercial banks, the PSBC and joint-stock commercial banks, the committee held the first plenary meeting and adopted the **Opinions of** **the High-level Banking Consumer Protection Steering Committee on Implementing the "Prevention First" Concept,** the **Opinions on the Implementation of Financial Literacy Programs by Banking Institutions,** and the **Implementation Plan on Standardizing Service Languages and Processes of the Banking Outlets.**

◎ Actively responding to consumer queries

The CBRC Public Education acted as the bridge for communication with the public and provided the public with convenient access to financial regulations and banking knowledge. In 2014, it was open for 224 days and received 7,139 calls and visits and responded to 2,367 queries made by individuals and organizations.

The Public Education staff responded to telephone query.

The Public Education held a financial literacy event.

◎ The China Banking Association strengthened self–regulation in respect of consumer protection

In 2014, the China Banking Association (CBA) led the effort to develop the **Normative Guidelines of China's Banking Industry for Public Education Services and Work** and the **Self-Regulatory Guidelines of China's Banking Industry for the Development of Accessible E-facilities**, guiding member banks to carry out consumer education events in accordance with laws and regulations, and incorporate consumer education into their development strategy, corporate culture and daily operations. These guidelines further define the standards for the development and renovation of accessible E-facilities, thereby improving the industry's capability to serve people with disabilities.

◎ The CBRC Hebei Office has largely built the consumer protection system

In April, the CBRC Hebei Office issued the *Detailed Implementation Rules of the CBRC Hebei Office for the Handling of Consumer Complaints* and other applicable rules, guiding supervisory authorities and banking institutions to regulate the operation procedures and improve working efficiency. A "three-in-one" (i.e. consumer education, financial literacy and dispute mediation) consumer protection framework has largely taken shape.

II. Promoting banking institutions to fulfill their duties

In 2014, the CBRC gave equal priority to conduct supervision and risk-based supervision, and guided banking institutions to promote the protection of consumers, thus fully enhancing the effectiveness of consumer protection.

Firstly, the CBRC encouraged banking institutions to further improve the consumer protection rules and system, develop consumer protection policies, improve the overarching design for consumer protection, and incorporate consumer protection into the board's roles and responsibilities. Secondly, it guided banking institutions to develop specific appraisal indicators and include consumer protection into their performance appraisal system, thus effectively boosting consumer protection through performance appraisal. Thirdly, it organized banking institutions to roll out the "National Financial Education" and "Financial Knowledge to Countryside" campaigns and set up a "Public Education Zone" in their outlets as an important platform for the promotion of financial literacy. Fourthly, the CBRC promoted the standardization of service processes and service languages in the banking industry with a view to improving the level of service. Fifthly, it guided banking institutions to improve the facilities for providing basic financial services at village level and continuously boost the building of credit culture at village level. Sixthly, it guided the CBA to improve banking institutions' capability to provide financial services for people with disabilities by developing industry norms and conventions, organizing campaigns for the protection of people with disabilities, and boosting the development of accessible facilities.

◎ BoCom actively improved consumer protection

In 2014, BOCom issued the *Consumer Protection Policy of BOCom,* the *Rules of BOCom for the Management of Consumer Protection*, and the *Consumer Protection Contingency Plan of BOCom.* These policies and rules helped to improve the top-level design for consumer protection with regard to management rules, infringement handling and internal appraisal and evaluation. All the requirements of supervisory authorities and industry association regarding consumer protection have been properly implemented.

III. Promoting financial literacy

In 2014, the CBRC strengthened the coordinated planning, established and improved the long-term mechanism for financial literacy promotion, gradually expanded the coverage of financial literacy promotion programs, and improved people's financial awareness and ability to protect their rights in accordance with law, thus improving people's financial competence.

1. Building the publicity brand

In September, the CBRC continued to roll out the National Financial Education Campaign in September, making it a brand of the CBRC and the banking industry in fulfilling social responsibilities and promoting financial literacy. The campaign involved over 210,000 banking outlets and about 1.44 million employees. Around 120,000 outdoor publicity booths were set up, offering over 94 million pieces of advice, distributing 110 million leaflets, sending about 180 million pieces of text messages, placing 160,000 publicity adverts, and generating around 29,000 media stories.

2. Enriching publicity tools

In 2014, with a view to providing the public with more convenient tools for learning financial knowledge, the CBRC organized and planned the production of motion pictures and cartoons about financial knowledge, designed children's wealth management diary, and launched the "Financial Manager" App. In addition, it compiled special editions of the Banking and Financial Literacy Guide for children and youth based on the cognitive ability and actual needs of children and young readers.

Banking and Financial Literacy Guide for Children and Youth compiled by the CBRC.

3. Innovating means of publicity

In 2014, the CBRC created more channels for publicizing financial knowledge and held different education and publicity activities for different groups of people. Before the 2014 FIFA World Cup started, some schools in about 10 provinces (municipalities/autonomous regions) held students' football contest under the theme of financial management. The contest combined football and financial knowledge. In Beijing, Shanghai, Chongqing, Anhui, Jiangsu and Liaoning financial management football game experience zones were built and open to the public free of charge. In Beijing, the "Drama" project was launched, producing anti-fraud dramas

The CBRC financial literacy publicity volunteers taught lessons to pupils.

123

to spread financial knowledge to the elderly. In Shanghai, the "Financial Knowledge to Campus" campaign was rolled out, during which financial quiz shows and debating contests were held.

Box 29 The CBRC strengthened the financial literacy publicity in rural areas

In August, the CBRC issued the *Guiding Opinions on Deepening the "Financial Knowledge to Countryside" Campaign.* A range of sustained, brand-oriented working carriers that were easy to accept and promote were devised according to the actual needs of rural consumers of financial services, including, 1) Financial Broadcasting Station, to cooperate with county, township/town radio channels and/or broadcasting stations to launch radio programs focusing on rural financial knowledge; 2) Financial TV Collection, to produce and launch customized popular and vernacular TV programs; 3) Financial Reading Center, to build rural reading centers equipped with facilities to view, read and listen to audio, visual and electronic materials.; 4) Financial Lecture Hall, to offer financial courses and training sessions in partnership with county-based radio and TV universities, employment training centers and agricultural science education bases; 5) Instant Financial Messaging, to publicize financial knowledge by means of website, text message, weibo, WeChat, etc..

◎ The CBRC Tianjin Office established the "Tianjin Banking Consumer Education Website"

Fully leveraging the Internet, the Tianjin Banking Consumer Education Website helps banking consumers to obtain resources and plan and manage their finance and investment. The website offers a full range of functions, including financial knowledge learning, online quiz show, topical financial issues, practical tools, consumer survey, etc.. It is a one-stop platform for publishing financial knowledge and information and engaging consumers and youngsters in particular.

◎ "Financial Evening School" became a new business card of Guizhou Rural Credit Union

In 2014, rural credit cooperatives in Guizhou's Qiannan Prefecture held financial evening schools in villages to publicize financial knowledge to farmers and teach them to handle transactions. As of end-2014, the Qiannan Office of Guizhou Rural Credit Union held 3,907 sessions of financial evening school for 228,700 participants, distributing over 240,000 leaflets, covering 95% of the towns/townships and 79% of the villages, and solving 1,267 issues on site for the farmers.

Financial Evening School of Sandu Rural Credit Union.

IV. Strengthening consumer protection survey and research

In 2014, the CBRC conducted China's first banking consumer protection survey. The survey covered consumers' basic information and financial consumption habits, banking products and services, level of financial literacy and complaints handling. Through the survey, the CBRC obtained further understanding of banking consumers' behaviors in selecting financial products and their financial capability. The survey findings would be helpful to building the banking consumer protection database, analyzing and assessing the status of consumer protection, thus constantly improving the relevance and effectiveness of consumer protection. The CBRC also carried out ad hoc research on the following issues, including, misleading sales of wealth management products, insufficient information disclosure in sales of bancassurance products, and blind spots in the banking outlet management and operations. Based on the research findings, the CBRC developed supervisory requirements for regulating the management and operation of banking institutions. It published the *Collection of International Financial Consumer Protection Laws and Regulations,* aiming to introduce international philosophies and practices regarding financial consumer protection. It compiled the *2013 Annual Report on Banking Consumer Protection in China,* aiming to extensively publicizing China's theoretical explorations and practical experiences in the promotion of consumer protection.

Photograph by the CBRC staff

Part Seven

Strengthening Transparency and Market Discipline

- Enhancing information disclosure
- Improving transparency of the banking sector
- Strengthening market discipline

I. Enhancing information disclosure

1. Improving the channel and platform of information disclosure

In 2014, the CBRC continued to strengthen the construction and management of its official website, regulate the information collection, review and release on the website, improve the information release appraisal mechanism, and fully leverage the information disclosure column on the website. By urging its departments and local offices to publish information in a timely and accurate manner and upgrading the frequency and quantity of information disclosure, the CBRC brought the official website into play and increased the transparency of the CBRC in fulfilling its duties.

2. Comprehensive work on information disclosure

(1) Fulfilling the duty of information disclosure. In 2014, the CBRC released to banking institutions 1,757 pieces of information about regulatory rules and documents, 647 pieces of information about regulations and policies, 289 pieces of information about licensing, supervisory and penalty procedures, 22,751 pieces of information about administrative approvals and penalty decisions, and 517 pieces of opinions and self-disciplinary policies of the CBRC and its local offices. In 2014, the official website of the CBRC published altogether 23,007 pieces of information, up by 6,270 pieces or 37.46 percent year-on-year, with clicks amounting to about 11,500.

(2) Proactive information disclosure. Firstly, the CBRC regularly released statistical information about supervisory policies and events through news media. It established the publicity system to announce regulatory & statistical information release date in advance, expanded the coverage of information disclosure, made detailed clarification of the dimensions to be disclosed, and strengthened the development of information transparency. Secondly, it made information disclosure in a proactive manner. It continued to release information about major decisions, events and supervisory developments and responded to public concerns through news media. It insisted on the news briefing system by holding press conferences for foreign journalists and media workshops, and strengthening communication with the media. It attended important forums and workshops and accepted interviews by major websites, providing official interpretations to topical issues and interacting with netizens. In 2014, the CBRC accepted approximately 2,000 interview requests by domestic and foreign journalists. To address the widely concerned hot topics, the CBRC organized 6 field trips with the participation of journalists, held 18 press briefings or conferences, and released 230 pieces of interpretation and response on its official website. Thirdly, it enhanced the disclosure of governmental information. In 2014, it made public 12,820 pieces of government information. The Government Information Disclosure Request Processing Form was made available online, and the "Platform for Disclosing Government Information upon Requests" was set up on the intranet to improve the disclosure efficiency. It released 4 quarterly Reports on the Performance of China's Banking Sector on its official website, edited and published the Statistical Yearbook of China's Commercial Banks.

(3) Information disclosure upon request. In 2014, the CBRC accepted 306 legitimate requests for government information disclosure, all of which were responded and replied.

Heads of relevant CBRC departments responded to issues of public concern during media interviews.

II. Improving transparency of the banking sector

Since its establishment, the CBRC issued a number of policy documents, including the *Guidelines on the Disclosure of Capital Adequacy Ratio Information by Commercial Banks*, the *Guidelines on the Information Disclosure of Financing Guarantee Companies*, and the *Provisional Rules Governing the Information Disclosure of Trust Investment Companies*, providing for detailed rules concerning the banking institutions' development of information disclosure mechanisms, and urging them to expand the coverage of information disclosure and improve the quality thereof on the basis of implementing the *Provisional Rules on Information Disclosure of Commercial Banks*. In 2014, it issued the *Guidelines on Disclosing Assessment Indicators of Global Systemic Importance of Commercial Banks*, requiring eligible commercial banks to disclose assessment indicators of global systemic importance from 2014 and thereby integrate into international supervisory rules regarding transparency.

Guided by the CBRC and based on their information disclosure polices, banking institutions disclosed information by making public announcement at operating premises and through official website, publicity materials, annual reports, CSR reports, news media, performance roadshow and responses to consumer inquiries. As a result, the breadth and depth of information disclosure was enhanced.

III. Strengthening market discipline

The CBRC is committed to urging the banking associations, trustee associations, finance companies association and financing guarantee companies association to fulfill their duties, establish and improve self-disciplinary mechanisms, and perform the functions of coordination, self-discipline and rights protection as self-disciplinary organizations.

In 2014, the China Banking Association (CBA) issued, for the seventh year in a row, the *Report on the Service Improvement of China's Banking Industry*. The CBA issued the *Self-disciplinary Guidelines for Trade Finance Business of Banking Institutions in China*, developed and issued the ***Basic Risk Assessment Questionnaire for Wealth Management Customers of Commercial Banks*** and the ***Sample Publicity Document for Wealth Management Products of Commercial Banks***. It inspected the implementation of a range of trade conventions, including the ***Evaluation Criteria for the Delivery of Standardized Services by Banking Outlets*** (CBSS1000). It further strengthened market discipline, improved members' awareness of implementing trade conventions and codes, and maintained a fair and orderly market. The China Trustee Association published the first ***Report on the Development of China's Trust Industry,*** and issued the ***Classification and Codes of Trust Businesses*** (JR/T 0106—2014) and the ***Sample Document for Collective Fund Trust Plan*** (JR/T 0077—2014). The China Trust Protection Fund Co., Ltd. was set up under the joint initiative of 13 trust companies led by the CTA, which further improved the mechanism for safeguarding the trust industry. The China National Association of Finance Companies set up a research taskforce to study the corporate governance of finance companies and published the ***Survey Report on Corporate Governance of Finance Companies***. It called upon the supervisory boards to oversee and inspect the implementation of trade rules, codes and norms, thereby facilitating the implementation of self-disciplinary regulations. The China Financing Guarantee Companies Association set up the self-disciplinary committee. It promoted the members-based information disclosure mechanism, and tried to regularly develop statistical statements and research reports. Preparatory work was done to establish the Micro Credit Companies Association and develop the ***Rules Governing Micro Credit Companies*** for regulating their development.

Photograph by the CBRC staff

Part Eight

Social Responsibility

- Guiding banking institutions to strengthen CSR
- Promoting the sustainable development of student loans
- Securing quality financial services during public holidays
- Supporting disaster relief and post-disaster reconstruction
- Supporting charity and poverty-stricken areas

I. Guiding banking institutions to strengthen CSR

The CBRC attached great importance to the fulfillment of social responsibilities by banking institutions. It encouraged them to engage in corporate social responsibilities (CSR) activities and release CSR reports regularly. In 2014, it encouraged banking institutions to perform their social responsibilities and regulated and supervised the performance. With the support from the CBRC, the CBA published, for six years in a row, the *Social Responsibility Report of the China's Banking Sector*.

The CBRC urged large commercial banks to prepare CRS reports in accordance with the *Opinions on Social Responsibility of Banking Institutions*, the *CSR Guidelines for China's Banking Institutions* and the requirements on CSR information disclosure of listed companies, and publish such reports after being authenticated by international accounting firms.

II. Promoting the sustainable development of student loans

In 2014, the CBRC continued to guide and encourage banking institutions to offer student loans. Firstly, the credit support was strengthened. The CBRC issued the *Notice on Adjusting and Improving Relevant Policies and Measures concerning National Student Loans* (Cai Jiao [2014] No. 180) jointly with the Ministry of Finance and the PBC, urging banking institutions to relax the loan application criteria. Secondly, the coverage of loans was expanded. The number of provinces and regions with access to such loans was increasing. More national and provincial-level impoverished counties, concentrated backward region belt and disaster stricken areas were included. Thirdly, efforts were made to improve the lending efficiency and simplify the loan application, approval and repayment processes. IT systems were built to improve the lending efficiency and the information management and consulting services concerning student assistance loans were improved. Fourthly, supporting service was improved. Actions were taken to promote employment and business start-ups among college graduates so as to address the high NPL ratio resulted from low employment rate.

◎ Promoting financial services to support employment and business creation of college graduates

Jointly with the Central Committee of the Communist Young League, the CBRC issued the *Notice on Further Promoting Financial Services to Support Employment and Business Creation of College Graduates* to all financial institutions across China, requiring the youth league organizations at all levels to strengthen the financial knowledge publicity and education for college students through mobile phone terminals, WeChat and other media and thereby help them to improve their awareness of finance and integrity. The *Notice* also requires the financial institutions to develop explorative and innovative financial products and services in light of college graduates' needs in business creation. They are required to, in line with the principle of keeping risks controllable and facilitating accessibility to favorable policies, improve the quality and intensity of financial services in support of employment and business creation by easing the lending criteria, optimizing loan approval process and setting up green channel for loan approval. According to the *Notice*, the youth league organizations are called upon to guide young financial employees to fulfill their social responsibilities, boost the development of financial inclusion, support the employment and business creation of young people, thereby promoting the employment and economic and social harmony.

III. Securing quality financial services during public holidays

The CBRC attached great importance to the delivery of financial services during important events, such as the APEC summit in Beijing and Nanjing 2014 Youth Olympic Games. Prior to the APEC summit, it issued the *Notice on Improving the Financial Services during the APEC Meeting*, requiring banking institutions to improve the quality of foreign-related financial services and contingency response capability and ensure the delivery of financial services during the summit. While the summit was held in Beijing, around 100 banking outlets in Beijing extended the "business hours", and banking institutions prepared cash in multiple currencies, developed contingency plans for collapse of self-service equipment, communication lines and other hardware, and established the fast-track channel for handling failure of communication lines.

For the Chinese New Year, National Day Holiday and other major public holidays, the CBRC issued notices in advance requiring banking institutions to ensure the continued delivery of financial services during the holidays, improve the quality of financial services and public satisfaction, ensure the safe operations of banking outlets, make sound arrangement of work shifts during holidays, contingency planning and premise security, and guard against fraud during holidays and issue risk alerts timely.

Box 30   Large commercial banks ensuring the continued delivery of financial services during the Chinese New Year holiday

During the Chinese New Year holiday in 2014, five large commercial banks took a range of measures to ensure the continued delivery of financial services and thereby met the public's needs for financial services. During the holiday, all banking outlets performed well on the whole. The telephone banking, online banking and ATM systems worked stably. There was no occurrence of major crimes or safety incidents.

Firstly, large banks used multiple channels to meeting people's need for financial services. During the holiday, 51,093 outlets of large banks were open as usual, accounting for 75.59% of the total. In key shopping areas, 100% outlets were open as usual. Altogether 341,610 self-service machines were in normal operation, accounting for 99.21% of the total. At the same time, other e-banking channels, such as telephone, Internet and cellphone banking, were used to provide around-the-clock financial services, thereby ensuring the timely processing of capital withdrawal, currency conversion, transfer, etc.. For example, the transaction value of the ICBC via

counter, self-service facilities and POS machines amounted to RMB 267.851 billion during the holiday. Secondly, the quality of financial services was improved. Tailored services were provided for migrant workers returning to hometowns, farmers and tourists. For example, some branches of the ABC set up windows for changing new bank notes and prepared large inventory of new bank notes. Some county-based outlets set up windows for returned migrant workers. The BOC offered settlement fee discount for returned migrant workers. Some BOCom outlets in scenic spots sent trip route reminders and other messages for its customers. The ICBC provided favorable capital settlement services for large growers, farmers and agro- and sideline products sellers, and offered discount for the purchase of agro-related products from UnionPay partners.

Thirdly, efforts were made to strengthen the dispatching of funds and prevention of operational risk. During the Chinese New Year holiday, large banks increased the frequency of fund dispatching and cash replenishment of self-service facilities in hotels, restaurants and shopping malls. In the mean time, branches and sub-branches were required to check all key aspects and departments so as to eliminate potential risks and ensure the safe operation of funds during the holiday. For example, the ABC sent 148 inspection teams consisting of around 600 staff to carry out safety inspection during the holiday. The inspection covered 50 centralized operation centers, 70 tier-2 branches, 144 tier-1 sub-branches, 500 outlets, 120 vaults and 288 detached self-service banks.

Fourthly, customer complaints and queries were handled properly in a timely manner. During the holiday, the Call Centers of large banks received 4,357,900 calls and accepted 827 complaints , of which 865 had been handled and accounted for 99.20% of the total.

IV. Supporting disaster relief and post-disaster reconstruction

In 2014, the CBRC took a series of initiatives to guide banking institutions to support disaster relief and post-disaster reconstruction endeavors, covering the earthquake-hit Ya'an and Kangding of Sichuan Province and Yingjiang, Jinggu and Ludian of Yunnan Province, severe flood-stricken areas of Jiangxi, Hunan, Guangdong, Guangxi and Guizhou, and Typhoon Rammasun-ravaged areas, etc..

◎ Supporting post–disaster reconstruction of Ya'an

Since April 20 2013 when the 7.0-magnitude earthquake hit Lushan County in Ya'an, Sichuan Province, banking institutions in quake-stricken areas continued to increase the scale of loan extension. As of end-2014, the loans in support of post-disaster reconstruction amounted to RMB21.725 billion, of which RMB12.26 billion was extended in 2014. The production and reconstruction of important infrastructures and livelihood-related projects were effectively supported, including electricity, communication, highway, transportation, water supply, gas supply, and etc..

◎ Providing financial services to support the disaster rescue and relief in the wake of the 6.5–magnitude earthquake in Ludian of Yunnan Province

After the earthquake occurred, the CBRC Yunnan office issued the *Emergent Notice on Providing Financial Services to Support the Disaster Rescue and Relief in Ludian*, guiding banking institutions in the earthquake-hit areas to provide contingent financial services by setting up mobile outlets and tent banks and carry out manual bookkeeping, etc.. Banking institutions provided certain preferential policies. For example, the account query fees, replacement fees and disaster relief fund transfer fees were exempted; one-on-one services were provided for severely stricken

Yunnan Rural Credit Union set up tent banks to secure non-stop delivery of financial services in Longtoushan Town (epicenter) after Ludian Earthquake occurred.

families; as for organizations and individuals failing to make timely repayments due to the disaster, banks did not urge the repayment, impose penalties or make bad credit record; and loans were allowed to be rolled over where appropriate. Local banking institutions were guided to provide financial services for post-disaster reconstruction, with a total credit line of RMB6.3 billion for reconstruction granted, a value of RMB700 million loans extended to farming households, a value of RMB300 million to MSEs, and a value of RMB1 billion loans to infrastructural projects. Under the guidance of the Yunnan Financial Trade Union, the banking institution in the province donated over RMB130 million to support disaster relief and post-disaster reconstruction.

◎ Banking institutions and trade associations actively supported disaster rescue and relief efforts

The China Trustee Association engaged the Sichuan Trust to establish the Designated Donation Trust Plan of Sichuan Trust with the donated funds of RMB18.86 million from the banking institutions. In addition, the China Trust Charity Fund was created under the Sichuan Charity Federation. In August 2014, a value of RMB3 million from charitable giving was used to support the charity program of "Financial Aid for 1,000 Students".

In 2014, the CCB donated RMB5 million to support the disaster relief and post-disaster reconstruction in the quake-hit areas in Ludian of Yunnan Province. It provided RMB3 million to the typhoon-striken Haikou City and other areas in Hainan Province. It gave NTD3 million to Kaohsiung after the gas explosion accident. It disbursed RMB7 million to the Mother Care Express Program for the purchase of 45 vans in Xinjiang, Tibet, Inner Mongolia, Liaoning and Hebei. The CCB has cumulatively donated RMB22 million to this program for the purchase of 146 vans. These vans are now active in 10 provinces, including Gansu, Qinghai, Xinjiang, Yunnan, Guangxi, Guizhou, Tibet, Inner Mongolia, Liaoning and Hebei. They are used to provide free pick-up and transfer of pregnant women and emergency patients, publicize knowledge on health care, and offer door-to-door services and free medical diagnosis for pregnant and delivering women. Local residents called them "life-saving vans".

In 2014, China EximBank sponsored ethnic minority teachers and students from Qoqek Prefecture to participate in a summer camp in Beijing and helped the Mandarin Primary School (all subjects are taught in Madarin) in Yimamu Township of Uqturqan County to solve their financial difficulty. It donated RMB3 million to quake-hit areas in Ludian of Yunnan Province, and its employees donated RMB480,000. It sent middle management officers to work on coordination of poverty-alleviation efforts in Minxian County, and financed the construction of 165 health care stations there (all completed) of which 85 had been put into use. It provided in-kind donations worth RMB70,000 and donated 50 computers to Minxian County through China Women's Development Foundation. It also organized young employees to provide volunteer services in Minxian County.

V. Supporting charity and poverty-stricken areas

The CBRC was actively involved in charitable activities. It encouraged its employees across the country to make donations to help students and take part in the "Financial Knowledge to Countryside" campaign. It encouraged the officers to enhance the sense of duty and mission and make more contributions. In 2014, the CBRC donated RMB3.85 million to poverty-stricken areas and undertakings such as poverty alleviation, students aid and disaster relief.

Box 31 The CBRC launched "5 Ones" initiative for young financial employees to help people with disabilities

In light of the special need of people with disabilities for financial services, the CBRC launched the "5 Ones" initiative to engage young financial employees to support people with disabilities. It published a letter to call upon everyone to support vulnerable groups, promote financial inclusion and provide quality services. It also produced public service ads which were broadcast on 9 channels of China Central Television. It started a "Darkness Challenge – Caring People with Disabilities" event on the Internet, calling on people to experience one minute of darkness. This event attracted over 100 million readers. A number of celebrities participated, including Lang Lang, Hai Xia, Zhu Xun and Ning Zetao. Around 1,000 pieces of videos were shared on the Internet.

Photograph by the CBRC staff

Photograph by the CBRC staff

Part Nine

Outlook

- Economic and financial outlook
- Supervisory focuses in 2015

I. Economic and financial outlook

Looking into the year of 2015, the development of world economy would still be dominated by deep adjustment after the global financial crisis, with continued track of slow recovery. The US economy is expected to maintain sound growth with monetary policy gradually normalized, but the pace and steps of interest hike are uncertain. The EU's economic outlook is not optimistic. Given the high deflationary pressure, high unemployment rate and high debt ratio, the size and effect of EU's quantitative easing are yet to be observed. Japan will be implementing strong Abenomic stimulus policy and facing the conflict between weakened export and structural problems, so whether it can achieve the expected economic growth is quite uncertain. Emerging countries will continue to face the twin pressure of weak growth dynamics and structural reform. India and China may have better growth than other emerging economies. The international financial and economic landscape may feature a new normal of slowed growth and high volatility.

Domestically, China's economic development has entered the new normal with growth moderating from high speed to mid-to-high speed. The focus of economic restructuring has shifted from expanding output and capacities to adjusting existing stock while enhancing the quality of the increment. The drivers for economic growth have shifted from conventional to new engines. Despite of difficulties and challenges, China still boasts important strategic opportunities, while its economy maintains positive growth momentum. Given the profound economic and financial changes, China's banking industry is confronted with increasingly complex risks. On one hand, some companies face operating difficulties, triggering exposures of credit risk. On the other hand, as China continues to advance the financial reform such as interest rate liberalization, together with the financial innovation made by Internet finance companies, the market is becoming increasingly competitive and risk control will become a more urgent yet challenging task for the banking industry.

II. Supervisory focuses in 2015

In 2015, the CBRC will continue to seek steady progress by guiding banking institutions to accurately understand and actively adapt to the new normal of economic development, accelerate the reform and transformation, firmly hold the bottom line of risk control, and advance the practice of ruling the banking industry according to law, thus improving the effectiveness of banking sector to serve the real economy.

1. Efforts will be made to improve the quality and efficiency of financial services. Banking institutions will be guided to leverage the strategic opportunities opened up by deepened international economic cooperation and national economic upgrading and transformation to provide well-targeted financial services with high added value to the real economy.

Firstly, providing support to the implementation of national strategies. Great efforts will be made to support the implementation of three major strategies, including the Belt and Road Initiative, coordinated development of Beijing, Tianjin and Hebei, and Yangtze River Economic Belt, facilitate the infrastructure development and investment for interconnectivity in Asian-Pacific region, and strengthen financial cooperation among BRICS. Innovations will be leveraged to facilitate the optimization and upgrading of national industrial structure. Credit will be tilted to support the development of infrastructure, key areas and weak aspects in the central and western part of China. The CBRC will actively participate in the negotiations on investment treaty and free trade zones, summarize and disseminate the successful experiences of the China (Shanghai) Pilot Free Trade Zone, and support the development of an open economy.

Secondly, efforts will be made to promote the industrial restructuring and actively identify and foster new engines of economic growth. Banking institutions will be guided to support the integration of new generation information technologies with modern manufacturing sector as well as technological innovation, innovation by all and independent innovation. Efforts will also be made to promote the renovation and upgrading of manufacturing and other conventional industries, boost the development of green, circular and low-carbon economy, and resolve the problem of excessive capacity. The transformation and upgrading of economic structure will be accelerated and more support will be given to strategic emerging industries and the services industry. Financial channels to increase residents' property income will be further expanded, with banks' wealth management business and trust business better regulated, so as to unleash the consumption potential, give full play to the roles of non-bank financial institutions, and facilitate the integration of industries and finance.

Thirdly, financial inclusion will be promoted. Banking institutions will be guided to extend more loans, issue more MSE financial bonds and agro-related financial bonds, and work hard to drive MSE loans and agro-related loans to grow at a rate higher than the average growth rate of all loans. The coverage of banking outlets will be expanded gradually so that financial institutions would cover all urban communities, villages and townships. The financial services for migrant workers, the unemployed and people with disabilities will be improved. The "Knowledge to Countryside" campaign will be further implemented, and financial consumer protection will be strengthened.

Fourthly, the cost of financing will be gradually driven down. Managerial innovations will be encouraged to reduce the cost of financing. To that end, unreasonable fees and charges will be eliminated and the financing chain will be shortened.

2. The responsibility of risk prevention and control will be earnestly fulfilled. In light of the major risks, banking institutions should become more forward-looking and sensitive in the course of risk prevention and control. They will be guided to strengthen the risk absorbing capability and firmly hold the bottom line of preventing systemic and regional risks, thus maintaining the robustness and soundness of the banking industry.

Firstly, banking institutions will prevent and resolve customer credit risks by understanding the customers, identifying potential risks and put them under control in a category-based manner. They will be guided to increase the risk response capability, strengthen the risk segregation, improve the practice of differentiated extension of credit, and avoid causing rupture of companies' capital chain as a result of withdrawing loans in a one-size-fits-all manner. Efforts will be made to enhance the interaction with local governments, judiciary authority, public security authority and trade associations for maintaining a sound credit environment.

Secondly, efforts will be made to resolve the risk of collateral value fluctuation. Banking institutions should dynamically check the composition of collaterals, strengthen related monitoring, analysis and early-warning, conduct dynamic stress testing, develop contingency plans, and strengthen collateral management and concentration management.

Thirdly, efforts will be made to prevent and resolve liquidity risks. Banking institutions should improve the liquidity monitoring and stress testing, and ensure that the liquidity management covers both on- and off-balance-sheet activities. They should also enrich liquidity management toolkit, improve the liquidity risk limit management, strengthen the liability management and evaluation and further optimize the structure of liability. The CBRC will strengthen inter-bank liquidity support and policy coordination, set up regional liquidity mutual assistance funds for small and medium-sized banks, strengthen cooperation between large banks and small and medium-sized banks, and establish inter-bank mutual assistance mechanism for maintaining market stability.

Fourthly, efforts will be made to resolve operational risks. The CBRC will maintain a high regulatory intensity in banking case prevention and control, strengthen the management of banking practitioners, establish the banking practitioner punishment information system, and strictly implement the employee management accountability. It will strengthen the IT risk supervision, accelerate the system renovation and upgrading, and carry out risk identification and contingency drills, thereby ensuring the safe operation of information systems.

Fifthly, efforts will be made to resolve the risk of private financing. Early risk prevention and control will be implemented to segregate the risk of private financing from the banking industry. Great efforts will be made to curb illegal fundraising, fight external encroachments, prevent misappropriation of credit funds for private financing, and protect the interests of banks from being encroached by collusion between staff and external parties. Banks should attach importance to reputational risk management and incorporate it into the comprehensive risk management system.

3. Endeavors will be made to deepen the banking reform and opening up. The CBRC will facilitate wider opening up of the financial industry, improve the banking business governance system and the supervisory regime, and consolidate the service infrastructure development, thereby sustaining the development of the banking industry.

Firstly, the CBRC will further encourage entry of private capital into the banking industry. In line with the guidance of the central government, the CBRC will actively facilitate relevant work on the promotion of establishing private banks; expand the pilot program of consumer finance company and extensively encourage eligible private capital to set up consumer finance companies; expand the proportion of private capital in village and township banks, support private capital to participate in or initiate the establishment of village banks, and increase the share of private capital; allow private capital to participate in the reorganization of more institutions; facilitate the equity diversification of the banking institutions, and create more channels for private capital to enter the banking industry.

Secondly, efforts will be made to promote the reform of banking operation structure and improve the specialized operation mechanism of banks. The reform will be further promoted to facilitate the shift of banking operations from department-based to process-based; the specialized business unit reform will be advanced to achieve appropriate integration of business activities, shorten the operating chain and reduce the management radius. Efforts will also be made to explore the reform of turning certain business segments and lines into subsidiaries.

Thirdly, the CBRC will actively promote the banking supervisory structure reform. It will continue to strengthen the effort to streamline administration and delegate power, explore the establishment of "three lists" (i.e. list of supervisory powers, list of supervisory duties, and negative list) and one website (i.e. the supervisory information website), improve the check-and-balance of supervisory power, make public the examination and approval process, and enhance supervisory transparency. The supervisory structure reform will be advanced to optimize the supervisory processes and allocation of supervisory resources, tilting more resources to central and key supervisory tasks. Efforts will be made to strengthen the in-process and ex-post supervision, improve on-site examination, explore the establishment of on-site examination department, and improve the quality of on-site examinations and capability to launch investigations and handle problems.

Fourthly, the CBRC will improve the development of service infrastructure and consolidate the following five systems, i.e., the product registration system with the focus on trust products, wealth management products and financial leasing products; the asset transfer system to facilitate normalized development of credit asset securitization; the liquidity mutual assistance system to serve the needs of small and medium-sized financial institutions for liquidity relief; the customer risk and fraud information system to enable sharing of customer risk information; and the news and information release system to form a centralized publication of banking news and information.

4. The CBRC will earnestly promote the rule of law. It will review the regulatory regime, accelerate efforts to check up regulations, facilitate the timely formulation, amendment and revoke of relevant regulations, and promote the rule of law from the four aspects of rule-making, enforcement, compliant operation and disciplinary punishment.

Firstly, it will improve the banking regulatory regime, facilitate the rule-making concerning market exit, financial inclusion and private financing, facilitate the amendment of a range of basic laws and regulations, and improve the administrative rules concerning liability business, wealth management business and off-balance-sheet businesses.

Secondly, it will improve the supervisory enforcement capacity, strictly perform supervisory duties, stringently define the enforcement responsibilities, and regulate the enforcement conduct. It will strengthen the building of the enforcement team and rule of law training, so as to improve the team's professional ability and ethics.

Thirdly, it will enhance the banking employees' awareness of compliance. Banking institutions should regulate business conducts, manage employees and protect consumer rights in accordance with law. By investigating into illegal actions and holding law breakers liable, the CBRC endeavor to increase the understanding, awareness and compliance of banking employees for compliant operations.

Fourthly, the CBRC will strengthen the disciplinary punishment. It will improve the working mechanism that separates investigation and punishment, explore the establishment of the administrative punishment committee, define the punishment procedures and criteria and regulate the administrative punishment conducts.

Part Ten

CBRC
Annual Report
2014

Appendixes

- Responsibility description of the CBRC departments and local offices
- Financial management activities of the CBRC
- Rules and regulatory documents issued in 2014
- MOUs and EOLs with overseas regulators
- Significant regulatory and supervisory events in 2014
- Terminology

Appendix 1 Responsibility description of the CBRC departments and local offices

I. Departments at the CBRC headquarters

1.General Office

Coordinate daily work of the CBRC head office; undertake a series of work including: drafting related documents, organizing and coordinating important meetings of the CBRC, confidentiality issues, secretariat function, documentation management, complaint handling, information processing, and ensuring the security of the office building, etc..

2.Policy Research Bureau

Undertake the top-level design, organization and implementation of further deepening reform and opening-up of the banking sector; follow and study the domestic and international macro-economies, financial situation, and the trend of financial policies, contact and coordinate with macroeconomic institutions and local governments, and lead the study on key policies of the banking sector serving the real economy; follow and study the international banking regulatory reform and trends of development, and conduct research on the regulatory framework, rules and regulations, and operational mechanism of the banking sector.

3.Prudential Regulation Bureau

Draft prudential regulation rules for banks and non-bank financial institutions, coordinate off-site surveillance work, and analyze and apply the off-site surveillance statistics; undertake identification, measurement, monitoring, analysis and reporting of systemic and regional risks of the banking sector, put forward measures and suggestions to control and mitigate risks, collect and compile various comprehensive supervisory returns, and disclose and share relevant statistical information.

4.On−site Examination Bureau

Formulate and implement on-site examination plans for various kinds of banks and non-bank financial institutions; coordinate the on-site examination work of the CBRC, set up and carry out on-site examination projects and make assessments afterwards; organize and coordinate comprehensive examinations of the banking sector and investigation of important cross-regional cases, investigate rule-breaking activities by banking institutions; guide and monitor CBRC local offices to conduct case investigation and on-site examination.

5.Legal Department

Draft and develop supervisory laws, administrative regulations, department rules, and normative documents, and provide proposals on new legislation or amendments to existing legislation; plan and coordinate the market entry work; coordinate and deal with legal affairs concerning banking development and supervision; make overall plans for supervision and examination on important issues involving financial security; be responsible for administrative appeals and lawsuits relating to CBRC regulatory decisions; be responsible for review of administrative penalties.

6.Financial Inclusion Department

Take the lead to coordinate and promote financial inclusion work by banking institutions, and provide guidance for CBRC local offices and local banking institutions; guide banking institutions to provide financial services for micro- and small-sized enterprises, for agriculture, rural areas and farmers, and for special groups of population; develop policy measures, operating rules and supervisory standards to promote sound development of financing guarantee institutions; coordinate the drafting of business regulatory measures and operating rules for micro-credit companies; study and develop supervisory measures and operating rules for P2P business.

7.Banking Information Technology Supervision Department

Oversee IT risks of banking institutions and provide relevant guidance; be responsible for the construction of IT system of the CBRC; manage and guide the IT supervision and IT development by CBRC local offices.

8.Banking Innovation Supervision Department

Develop implementation rules of prudential regulation on business and product innovation by banking institutions, and coordinate the functional supervision on financial innovation; conduct model analysis and risk surveillance on financial innovation by banking institutions; set the categories of products or services, scope, and participating institutions of banking innovation pilot programs; coordinate and cooperate with multiple ministries on financial innovation supervision; coordinate the supervision on banking service price, and put forward proposals for setting up on-site examination projects; follow the business development trend of domestic and foreign banking institutions, carry out relevant research and conduct exchange and communication.

9.Banking Consumer Protection Department

Develop the overall plan, guiding opinions, and implementation rules for banking consumer protection; provide guidance for banking institutions to carry out consumer protection; follow and study the trend of domestic and foreign banking consumer protection, and conduct cooperation and information exchange; respond to the complaints of financial consumers and those involving cross-market and cross-sectoral financial products or services within the scope of the CBRC's duties; plan, organize and coordinate with relevant CBRC departments and other institutions to launch banking consumer protection publicity and education programs, and take charge of the operation and management of the CBRC Public Education Center.

10.Policy Bank Supervision Department

Regulate and supervise the China Development Bank, Export-Import Bank of China, Agricultural Development Bank of China, and Postal Savings Bank of China (the first three banks are referred to as the "policy banks").

11.Large Commercial Bank Supervision Department

Regulate and supervise the Industrial and Commercial Bank of China, Agricultural Bank of China, Bank of China, China Construction Bank, and Bank of Communications.

12.National Joint-stock Commercial Bank Supervision Department

Regulate and supervise national joint-stock commercial banks, including the China CITIC Bank, China Guangfa Bank, Ping An Bank, China Merchants Bank, Shanghai Pudong Development Bank,

Industrial Bank, China Minsheng Banking Corporation, Evergrowing Bank, China Zheshang Bank and Bohai bank.

13.City Commercial Bank Supervision Department

Regulate and supervise city commercial banks and private banks.

14.Rural Financial Institution Supervision Department

Regulate and supervise medium and small-sized rural financial institutions, including rural credit cooperatives and credit unions, rural commercial banks, rural cooperative banks, and village and township banks.

15.Foreign Bank Supervision Department

Regulate and supervise foreign banking institutions, including wholly foreign-owned banks, Sino-foreign joint-venture banks, foreign bank branches and representative offices.

16.Trust Institution Supervision Department

Regulate and supervise trust institutions, including trust companies and the China Trust Protection Fund Corporation; provide guidance for the operation and management of the China Trust Protection Fund.

17.Non−bank Financial Institution Supervision Department

Regulate and supervise non-bank financial institutions, including financial asset management companies, finance companies affiliated to corporate groups, financial leasing companies, auto financing companies, consumer finance companies, and money brokerage firms; regulate and supervise representative offices of overseas non-bank financial institutions.

18.Anti−illegal Fund Raising Office (Banking Security & Safeguard Bureau)

Handle illegal-fund raising cases and safeguard the security of the banking sector.

19.Accounting Department

Manage internal financial work of the CBRC, prepare and report the annual financial budget and statement of the CBRC; manage work related to infrastructure development, government procurement and fixed assets; develop rules for the implementation of the accounting standards pertaining to the banking industry, review and approve the accounting policies and procedures of banking institutions, and oversee, guide and coordinate the accounting activities of banking institutions; coordinate the collection of supervision fees from banking institutions.

20.International Department (Office of Hong Kong and Macao & Taiwan Affairs)

Coordinate and manage the foreign affairs and overseas business visits of the CBRC; be responsible for cooperation and communication with overseas financial supervisory authorities and international financial institutions; be responsible for affairs in relation to Hong Kong, Macao SARs and Taiwan.

21.Staff Compliance & Disciplinary Bureau

Supervise and review the implementation of relevant rules and policies by the CBRC, assist in building a clean and honest government, and organize and coordinate anti-corruption work.

22.Human Resources Department

Develop rules and policies on the human resources management of the CBRC; undertake the human resources management work for the CBRC headquarters and local offices, undertake the management of senior management of selected banking institutions; assist in the staff training.

23.Publicity & Information Department

Be responsible for the cultural development, news and publicity, and public opinions management of the banking sector.

24. CBRC Headquarters CPC Committee

Be responsible for the CPC affairs at the CBRC headquarters.

25.Party School

Implement staff training plans, and organize theory training and supervisory affairs training.

26. CBRC Staff Union

Perform duties of the union, including protection, construction, participation and education, lead and organize staff unions of various levels within the CBRC system to carry out their work; represent and protect the legitimate rights of staff, and better serve the supervisory work.

27. Financial Youth League Committee

Be responsible for youth league affairs and youth affairs of the central financial system.

28.Headquarters Service Center

Provide logistics management and services at the CBRC headquarters.

II. CBRC local offices

1. Provincial offices

With the delegation from the CBRC head office, develop implementation rules for relevant supervisory regulations within their jurisdictions; conduct regulation over the establishment, changes, termination and business activities of the banking institutions and their branches within their jurisdictions; issue penalties against illegal and rule-breaking banking activities; review the qualifications of senior executives of banking institutions under their jurisdictions; provide relevant statistical data and information within their jurisdictions; be responsible for human resources management of their offices.

2. Field offices at the cities specially designated in the state plan

With the delegation from the CBRC head office, develop implementation rules for relevant supervisory regulations within their jurisdictions; conduct regulation over the establishment, change, termination and business activities of the banking institutions and their branches within their jurisdictions; issue penalties against illegal and rule-breaking banking activities; review the qualifications of senior executives of banking institutions within their jurisdictions; provide relevant statistical data and information within their jurisdictions; be responsible for human resources management of their offices.

3. Field offices

With the delegation from the CBRC head office and provincial offices, conduct regulation over the establishment, change, termination and business activities of the banking institutions and their branches within their jurisdictions; issue penalties against illegal and rule-breaking banking activities; review the qualifications of senior executives of banking institutions within their jurisdictions; conduct supervision over local UCCs, RCCs and credit unions in counties without local supervisory agencies, provide relevant statistical data and information within their jurisdictions; be responsible for human resources management of their offices.

With the delegation from the provincial or field offices, local supervisory agencies in counties are responsible for supervising local banking institutions, UCCs, RCCs and credit unions; collect information about local financial risks and report to upper-level CBRC offices.

Appendix 2   Financial management activities of the CBRC

According to the relevant rules and policies issued by the MOF, the CBRC collects supervision fees from banking institutions, which are directly contributed to the treasury, while the annual budget of the CBRC is determined and allocated by the MOF.

Starting from 2004, the CBRC has collected supervision fees (institutional supervision fee and business supervision fee) from commercial banks of various kinds, policy banks and the CDB, urban and rural credit cooperatives, trust companies, finance companies, financial leasing companies, postal savings bank, banking asset management companies and other banking institutions. In 2014, the institutional supervision fee is charged at 0.05 percent of the paid-up capital of each banking institution at the end of the previous year while taking into account the institution's risk performance. The business supervision fee is charged under a progressive system (divided into different tranches depending on the level of total assets excluding paid-up capital at the end of the previous year) and by taking into accounts the risk performance. Specifically, the business supervision fee = (total assets – paid-up capital) × rate for corresponding tranches × risk-adjusted factor – supervision fee charged by the host country supervisors on the institution's overseas operations. The banking supervision fee is listed into the fiscal budgets and submitted directly into treasury. The MOF designates its local officers to oversee the collection of supervision fees by the CBRC.

Starting from 2004, the CBRC has budgeted its expenses in the same way as other central government agencies. The annual expenditure usually consists of a basic expenditure budget and project expenditure budget. Basic expenditure budget is mainly used to fund the routine operations and supervisory activities of the CBRC and its local offices. Project expenditure budget is mainly used to fund specific projects such as office renovation, purchase of office supplies and vehicles, purchase of IT equipment and the special inspection taskforce. Since the adoption of such budgeting practices, the CBRC has developed and strictly enforced relevant financial management rules to secure strong financial support for supervisory activities. The underlying objectives for its financial management activities are to properly allocate its financial budget funds, utilize supervisory resources in a cost-efficient manner, and proactively improve the supervisory infrastructure and employees' benefits in a cost effective, people-oriented and thrifty manner.

Appendix 3   Rules and regulatory documents issued in 2014

Rules

Decree of the CBRC, No.1, 2014	*Rules on Service Charges of Commercial Banks*, issued on February 14, 2014
Decree of the CBRC, No.2, 2014	*Rules on Liquidity Risk Management of Commercial Banks (Provisional)*, issued on January 17, 2014
Decree of the CBRC, No.3, 2014	*Rules governing Financial Leasing Companies*, issued on March 13, 2014
Decree of the CBRC, No.4, 2014	*Implementation Rules on Administrative Licensing of Small- and Medium-sized Financial Institutions in Rural Areas*, issued on March 13, 2014
Decree of the CBRC, No.5, 2014	*Provisional Rules on Factoring Business of Commercial Banks*, issued on April 3, 2014
Decree of the CBRC, No.6, 2014	*Implementation Rules on Administrative Licensing of Foreign-funded Banks*, issued on September 11, 2014

Regulatory Documents

Yin Jian Fa No.1, 2014	*Notice of CBRC on Issuing the Guidelines on Disclosing Assessment Indicators of Global Systemic Importance of Commercial Banks* , issued on January 3, 2014
Yin Jian Fa No.7, 2014	*Guiding Opinions of CBRC on Financial Services to Micro and Small Enterprises,* issued on March 13, 2014
Yin Jian Fa No.10, 2014	*Notice of CBRC and PBC on Promoting Business Cooperation between Commercial Banks and Third-party Payment Institutions,* issued on April 3, 2014
Yin Jian Fa No.12, 2014	*Guiding Opinions of CBRC and CSRC on Issuing Preferred Shares as Tier 1 Capital by Commercial Banks,* issued on April 3, 2014

Yin Jian Ban Fa No.140, 2014	*Notice of the CBRC General Office on Regulating Interbank Business of Commercial Banks*, issued on May 8, 2014
Yin Jian Fa No.32, 2014	*Notice of CBRC on Issuing the Guidelines on Supervisory Ratings of Commercial Banks*, issued on June 19, 2014
Yin Jian Ban Fa No.198, 2014	*Notice of the CBRC General Office on Issuing the Provisional Rules on Specialized Subsidiaries of Financial Leasing Companies*, issued on July 11, 2014
Yin Jian Fa No.36, 2014	*Notice on Improving and Innovating Micro and Small Enterprise Loan Services and Enhancing Financial Services for Micro and Small Enterprises*, issued on July 23, 2014
Yin Jian Fa No.37, 2014	*Notice of CBRC on Issuing the Measures on Assessing Consumer Protection Work of Banking Institutions (Provisional),* issued on August 6, 2014
Yin Jian Fa No. 40, 2014	*Notice of CBRC on Issuing the Guidelines on Internal Controls of Commercial Banks*, issued on September 12, 2014
Yin Jian Fa No.41, 2014	*Notice on Issuing the Rules on Supervision of Financial Asset Management Companies*, issued on October 14, 2014
Yin Jian Fa No.50, 2014	*Notice of CBRC and MOF on Issuing the Rules on Trust Security Fund*, issued on December 10, 2014
Fa Gai Jia Ge No.268, 2014	*Notice of NDRC and CBRC on issuing the Catalogue of Government Reference Price on Commercial Banks Services*, issued on February 14, 2014
Bo Jian Fa No.3, 2014	*Notice of CIRC and CBRC on Regulating Insurance Agency Business of Commercial Banks*, issued on January 8, 2014

Appendix 4 MOUs and EOLs with overseas regulators

	Overseas Regulators	Country/Region	Effective date
1	Monetary Authority of Macao	Macao SAR	August 22, 2003
2	Hong Kong Monetary Authority	Hong Kong SAR	August 25, 2003
3	Financial Services Authority	U.K.	December 10, 2003
4	Financial Supervisory Commission	Korea	February 3, 2004
5	Monetary Authority of Singapore	Singapore	May 14, 2004
6-1	Board of Governors of the Federal Reserve System (FED) Office of the Comptroller of the Currency (OCC) Federal Deposit Insurance Corporation (FDIC)	U.S.	June 17, 2004
6-2	California Department of Financial Institutions	U.S.	November 6, 2007
6-3	New York State Banking Department	U.S.	May 7, 2009
7	Office of the Superintendent of Financial Institutions Canada	Canada	August 13, 2004
8	National Bank of the Kyrgyz Republic	Kyrgyzstan	September 21, 2004
9	State Bank of Pakistan	Pakistan	October 15, 2004
10	Federal Financial Supervisory Authority (BaFin)	Germany	December 6, 2004
11	Commission for Banking Supervision of the Republic of Poland	Poland	February 27, 2005
12	Commission Bancaire	France	March 24, 2005
13	Australian Prudential Regulation Authority	Australia	May 23, 2005
14	Banca d' Italia	Italy	October 17, 2005
15	Bangko Sentral ng Pilipinas	The Philippines	October 18, 2005
16	Central Bank of the Russian Federation	Russia	November 3, 2005

Contined

	Overseas Regulators	Country/Region	Effective date
17	Hungarian Financial Supervisory Authority	Hungary	November 21, 2005
18	Banco de Espana	Spain	April 10, 2006
19	Jersey Financial Services Commission	Jersey	April 27, 2006
20	Banking Regulation and Supervision Agency of Turkey	Turkey	July 11, 2006
21	Bank of Thailand	Thailand	September 18, 2006
22	National Bank of Ukraine	Ukraine	January 30, 2007
23	National Bank of the Republic of Belarus	Belarus	April 23, 2007
24	Qatar Financial Centre Regulatory Authority	Qatar	May 11, 2007
25	Icelandic Financial Supervisory Authority	Iceland	June 11, 2007
26	Dubai Financial Services Authority	Dubai	September 24, 2007
27	Swiss Federal Banking Commission	Switzerland	September 29, 2007
28	De Nederlandsche Bank	Netherlands	December 25, 2007
29	Commission de Surveillance du Secteur Financier Luxemburg	Luxembourg	February 1, 2008
30	State Bank of Vietnam	Vietnam	May 5, 2008
31	Banking, Finance and Insurance Commission of Belgium	Belgium	September 25, 2008
32	Irish Financial Services Regulatory Authority	Ireland	October 23, 2008
33	Central Bank of Nigeria	Nigeria	February 6, 2009
34	Bank Negara Malaysia	Malaysia	November 11, 2009
35	Financial Supervisory Commission of Chinese Taipei	Taiwan	November 16, 2009
36	The Czech National Bank	Czech Republic	January 5, 2010
37	The Malta Financial Services Authority	Malta	February 2, 2010
38	Bank of Indonesia	Indonesia	July 15, 2010
39	The Bank Supervision Department of the South African Reserve Bank	South Africa	November 17, 2010
40	National Bank of Tajikistan	Tajikistan	November 25, 2010

Contined

	Overseas Regulators	Country/Region	Effective date
41	Reserve Bank of India	India	December 16, 2010
42	Central Bank of Cuba	Cuba	June 5, 2011
43	The Superintendency of Banks and Financial Institutions of Chile	Chile	June 9, 2011
44	The Central Bank of the United Arab Emirates	United Arab Emirates	July 13, 2011
45	The Central Bank of Cyprus	Cyprus	July 15, 2011
46	The Central Bank of Argentina (The Superintendence of Financial and Exchange Entities)	Argentina	October 5, 2011
47	Guernsey Financial Services Commission	Guernsey	November 15, 2011
48	Banco Central do Brasil	Brazil	June 21, 2012
49	National Bank of Cambodia	Cambodia	April 8, 2013
50	The Financial Supervision Commission of the Isle of Man	Isle of Man	April 15, 2013
51	Bank of Zambia	Zambia	April 25, 2013
52	Superintendencia de Servicios Financieros del Banco Central del Uruguay	Uruguay	May 27, 2013
53	The Supervisor of Banks at the Bank of Israel	Israel	May 27, 2013
54	The Central Bank of Bahrain	Bahrain	September 16, 2013
55	The National Bank of Kazakhstan	Kazakhstan	September 25, 2013
56	Bank of Ghana	Ghana	June 9, 2014
57	Finansinspektionen (Swedish Financial Supervisory Authority)	Sweden	June 25, 2014
58	The Bank of Mongolia	Mongolia	August 21, 2014
59	The Superintendence of Banking, Insurances and Private Pension Fund Administrators of Peru	Peru	October 10, 2014
60	Qatar Central Bank	Qatar	November 3, 2014

Appendix 5 Significant regulatory and supervisory events in 2014

On January 6-7	The CBRC held the 2014 National Banking Supervision Working Conference, which laid out the priorities for the year 2014.
On January 12	Chairman SHANG Fulin attended the meeting of Governors and Heads of Supervision (GHOS) in Basel, Switzerland.
On January 16	The CBRC held Non-bank Financial Institutions Supervision Working Conference.
On January 17	The CBRC issued the **Rules on Liquidity Risk Management of Commercial Banks (Provisional)**, aiming to improve policies for liquidity risk supervision, and establish a regulatory framework for liquidity risks.
On January 22	The CBRC held the 2014 Information Technology Working Conference.
On January 24	The CBRC held the Conference on Party Work-style and Clean Government Construction as well as Disciplinary Inspection.
On January 25-26	The 1st plenary session of the 2nd committee of All-China Financial Youth Federation was held.
On January 26	The CBRC held the National Conference on the Supervision of Large Banks.
On February 8	The **Notice on Improving Office Utilization** was issued.
On February 10	Chairman SHANG Fulin wrote an article titled **Creating a New Era of Reform and Opening Up in the Banking Sector** on the journal **ZiGuangGe**.
On February 13	The CBRC and the HKMA held the 19th supervisory dialogue in Beijing.
On February 14	Chairman SHANG Fulin met with Timothy Franz Geithner, former US Secretary of the Treasury.
On February 14	The CBRC and the National Development and Reform Commission (NDRC) jointly issued the **Rules on Service Charges of Commercial Banks**, which standardizes service prices of commercial banks and specified penalties against illegal pricing activities, aiming to protect the rights and interests of financial customers.

On March 10	The CBRC held the 2014 Conference on the Supervision of Small- and Medium-sized Rural Financial Institutions.
On March 11	Chairman SHANG Fulin attended the press conference on the 2nd session of the 12th NPC, and answered questions from the media about private bank pilot program, financial services, risk prevention and other topics.
On March 11	Chairman SHANG Fulin revealed the first 5 pilot private banks in his interview with the **People's Daily** which afterwards published a comment article titled "Cheers for the First Step in Deepening Financial Reform".
On March 11, June 10, September 22, December 2	The CBRC representatives attended the 151th, 152th, 153th and 154th plenary meetings of the BCBS in Basel, Switzerland.
On March 13	The CBRC revised and issued the **Rules Governing Financial Leasing Companies**, aiming to further promote the pilot program of setting up financial leasing companies by commercial banks and facilitate a sound development of the industry.
On March 13	The CBRC revised and issued the **Implementation Rules on Administrative Licensing of Rural Small- and Medium-sized Financial Institutions,** for the purpose of streamlining administration and delegating power and further improving market entry mechanism.
On March 13-14	The 7th China-US Banking Supervisory Dialogue was held in Beijing.
On March 17	The **Notice of the CBRC General Office on Further Enhancing Banking Service and Personnel Conduct Management** was released, urging commercial banks to strengthen internal management, regulate personnel behavior and effectively prevent private lending risks from transmitting into banks.
On March 24	Chairman SHANG Fulin met with Glenn Stevens, Governor of the Reserve Bank of Australia.
On March 25 - April 2	Chairman SHANG Fulin met with the Bank of France Governor Christian Noyer, the Central Bank of Ireland Governor Patrick Honohan and the Bank of England Governor Mark Carney respectively in France, Ireland and UK.
On March 25	The Inter-agency Anti-illegal Fund-raising Taskforce held a press conference and issued the **Opinions on Several Issues Concerning the Laws Applicable to the Trial of Criminal Cases Relating to Illegal Fund-raising,** launching the 2014 publicity and education campaign to guard and battle against illegal fund-raising.

On March 26	The CBRC issued the *Notice on Further Promoting Diligent and Cost-effective Working Style*.

On March 31	Chairman SHANG Fulin attended the FSB plenary meeting in London, UK.

On April 3	The CBRC issued the *Provisional Rules on Factoring Business of Commercial Banks*, which specifies requirements for factoring business in terms of corporate governance, insitutional building and internal control, aiming to promote the sound development of the factoring business of commercial banks.

On April 3	The CBRC and the CSRC jointly issued the *Guiding Opinions of the CBRC on Issuing Preferred Shares as Tier 1 Capital by Commercial Banks*, which specifies the qualification criteria for preferred shares to be taken as other Tier 1 capital of commercial banks.

On April 4	The Cross-agency Taskforce on Credit Guarantee held the first meeting.

On April 8	The CBRC issued the *Guiding Opinions on the Risk-based Supervision of Trust Companies*.

On April 10	In accordance with *the Capital Rules of Commercial Banks (Provisional)*, the six banks of ICBC, ABC, BOC, CCB, BOCom and were approved to adopt the advanced approach for capital management.

On April 24, May 28, October 11	Three documents were respectively released, namely: the *Notice on Regulating Interbank Business of Financial Institutions,* which was jointly issued by the CBRC, the PBC, the CSRC, the CIRC and the SAFE; the *Notice on Regulating the governance of Interbank Business of Commercial Banks*, which was designed as a supplementary policy document to further specify standards for interbank business of commercial banks; and, the *Notice on Conducting Special Examinations over the Implementation of the New Rules Concerning Interbank Business of Banking Institutions,* requiring banking institutions to carry out self-examination on the implementation of the new rules and laying out relevant on-site examination arrangements.

On April 29	The 2014 First Quarterly Working Conference on Economic and Financial Condition Analysis was held.

On May 5	The 2014 Annual Meeting of Finance Companies of Enterprise Groups was held in Wuhan, requiring finance companies to achieve sound development through improving the strategic investors cooperation mechanism, industry discipline mechanism, composite pricing mechanism, product innovation mechanism and stable remuneration mechanism.

On June 5	Chairman SHANG Fulin met with David Lipton, First Deputy Managing Director of the International Monetary Fund.
On June 5	The CBRC called on its staff to learn from LI Jianhua.
On June 6	The CBRC held a press conference on "Financial Sector to Serve the Real Economy" at the State Council Information Office, answering questions from the media on topics including lowering financing cost, resolving overcapacity, optimizing agro-related financial services and improving financial services for micro and small enterprises.
On June 16	The *Notice of the CBRC General Office on Relevant Issues Concerning Further Streamlining Administration, Delegating Power and Improving Market Access* was issued, aiming to ensure effective implementation of streamlining administration and delegating power to the local level.
On June 23	The CBRC issued the *Guidelines on Supervisory Ratings of Commercial Banks*, for the purpose of adjusting the rating system, enhancing comparison among homogeneous commercial banks and improving differentiated supervision.
On June 30	The CBRC issued the *Notice on Adjusting Loan-to-Deposit Calculation Methods*, which redefined the numerator and the denominator of the LTD ratio and adjusted the types of currencies concerned.
On July 7	Chairman SHANG Fulin met with Jim Yong Kim, President of the World Bank.
On July 9-10	Chairman SHANG Fulin attended the 6th China-US Strategic and Economic Dialogue.
On July 10	The CBRC issued the *Notice on Improving the Organization and Governance Structure of Wealth Management Businesses of Commercial Banks,* requiring banking institutions to conduct organizational reform for wealth management business and set up specific wealth management departments.
On July 10	Chairman SHANG Fulin met with Janet Yellen, Chair of the Board of Governors of the Federal Reserve System.
On July 23	The CBRC issued the *Notice on Improving and Innovating Micro and Small Enterprise Loan Services and Enhancing Financial Services for Micro and Small Enterprises*, encouraging banking institutions to improve and innovate loan services for micro and small enterprises, and enhancing the efficiency of loan services.

On July 25	The CBRC held the 2014 First Semi-annual Working Conference on Banking Supervision & National Economic and Financial Condition Analysis.
On July 25	The CBRC approved China Development Bank Housing Finance to launch business operation.
On July 29	Chairman SHANG Fulin met with Elke Konig, President of the Federal Financial Supervisory Authority (BaFin).
On August 3	The CBRC deployed financial services for earthquake relief work in Ludian County of Yunnan Province.
On September 11	The CBRC revised the *Implementation Rules on Administrative Licensing for Foreign Banking Institutions* and renamed it the *Implementation Rules on Administrative Licensing for Foreign-funded Banks.*
On September 12	The CBRC, the MOF and the PBC jointly issued the *Notice on Strengthening Deposit Deviation Management of Commercial Banks*, guiding commercial banks to design indicators for deposit deviation conditions, and further curbing irregular deposit-taking activities, especially at month/quarter end.
On September 12	The 6th Sino-British Economic and Financial Dialogue was held in Beijing.
On September 15	The 2nd China-France High Level Economic and Financial Dialogue was held in Paris.
On September 22-25	The 18th International Conference of Banking Supervisors (ICBS) was held. 250 representatives of 110 supervisory authorities and central banks from 93 countries and regions participated in the meeting, and discussed the role of finance in promoting economic growth and post-Basel III international regulatory reforms.
On September 24	The CBRC and the HKMA held the 20th supervisory dialogue in Tianjin.
On September 26	Chairman SHANG Fulin met with Muliaman Hadad, Chairman of the Financial Services Authority (OJK) of Indonesia.
On October 13	The CBRC, the MOF, the PBC, the CSRC and the CIRC jointly issued the *Rules on Supervision of Financial Asset Management Companies,* aiming to regulate the comprehensive businesses and internal controls of financial asset management companies at the group level.
On October 16	The 7th China-Canada Financial Policy Dialogue was held in Canada.

On October 17	The CBRC issued the *Notice of the CBRC General Office on Implementing the Implementation Rules on Administrative Licensing for Foreign-funded Banks.*
On October 24	The CBRC and the Supreme People's Court jointly issued the *Opinions on Conducting Network Inquiry and Control and Joint Credit Discipline by People's Courts and Banking Institutions*, aiming to jointly establish a network inquiry and control mechanism and a credit discipline mechanism.
On October 24	The CBRC and the Tibet Autonomous Region's Party committee and government jointly held a seminar focused on financial support for economic and social development in Tibet, analyzed the current problems and difficulties and proposed new measures to support the economic development of Tibet.
On November 4	Chairman SHANG Fulin met with John C Tsang, Financial Secretary of the HKSAR.
On November 13	The CPC Committee of the CBRC held a meeting to deliver the key decisions adopted at the Fourth Plenary Session of the 18th CPC Central Commission for Discipline Inspection.
On November 24, December 2, December 15	The CBRC respectively issued the *Notice to Encourage and Guide Private Capital to Participate in Ownership Reform of Rural Credit Cooperatives,* the *Guiding Opinions on Promoting the Sound Development of Village and Township Banks* and the *Supervisory Guidelines to Strengthen the Mechanism of Financial Services to Agriculture, Farmers and Rural Areas by Rural Commercial Banks.* With these efforts, the CBRC further clarified policy requirements for encouraging and guiding private capital to participate in ownership reform of rural credit cooperatives, improved policy support for the development of village and township banks, boosted the localization, privatization and professionalization of village and township banks, and accelerated the building-up of a long-term mechanism for financial services to agriculture, farmers, and rural areas.
On November 25	Chairman SHANG Fulin met with Queen Máxima of the Netherlands, the United Nations Secretary-General's Special Advocate for Inclusive Finance for Development (UNSGA).
On November 27	The *Decision of the State Council on Amending the Regulation of the People's Republic of China on Administration of Foreign-Funded Banks* was issued, which removed the requirements of the minimum working capital for branches of locally incorporated foreign banking institutions, removed the requirements of setting up representative offices before establishing operational banking institutions, and substantially lowered the threshold for foreign banking institutions to conduct RMB business.

On December 8	Chairman SHANG Fulin met with Michael Noonan, Minister for Finance of Ireland.
On December 10	The CBRC and the MOF jointly issued the *Rules on Trust Protection Fund.*
On December 12	Webank in Qianhai District of Shenzhen, the first pilot private bank, was approved by the CBRC to commence business operations.
On December 19	China Trust Protection Fund Co., Ltd. (CTPF) was founded with the approval from the State Council and the CBRC. CTPF is a banking institution subject to the supervision of CBRC and funded by the China Trustee Association along with 13 trust companies.
On December 23	The CBRC held the 2015 Working Conference on Banking Supervision, which laid out the priorities for the year 2015, and urged the banking sector to proactively adapt to the "new normal", push adhead with the reforms and opening up of the banking sector, improve the legal system of the financial sector, strengthen financial risk management, and upgrade capacity in serving the real economy.
On December 25	The Fourth Cross-Strait Consultation on Banking Supervision was held in Beijing, during which Chairman SHANG Fulin and ZENG Mingzong, Chairman of Financial Supervisory Commission of Chinese Taipei, discussed issues of common interest.

Appendix 6   Terminology

Terms	Coverage of institutions	Statistical coverage of institutions
Banking Institutions	Policy banks, large commercial banks, joint-stock commercial banks, city commercial banks, rural cooperative financial institutions, postal savings bank, banking asset management companies, foreign banks, Sino-German Bausparkasse, non-bank financial institutions, new-type rural financial institutions, and other types financial institutions under the CBRC's jurisdiction	Policy banks, large commercial banks, joint-stock commercial banks, city commercial banks, rural cooperative financial institutions, postal savings bank, foreign banks, Sino-German Bausparkasse, non-bank financial institutions, new-type rural financial institutions under the CBRC's jurisdiction (excluding private banks and China Trust Protection Fund Corporation)
Policy Banks	China Development Bank, the Export-Import Bank of China, Agricultural Development Bank of China	Same as institution coverage
Commercial Banks	large commercial banks, joint-stock commercial banks, city commercial bank, rural commercial banks and foreign banks	Same as institution coverage
Major Commercial Banks	large commercial banks and joint-stock commercial banks	Same as institution coverage
Large Commercial Banks	Industrial and Commercial Bank of China, Agricultural Bank of China, Bank of China, China Construction Bank, and Bank of Communications	Same as institution coverage
Small- and Medium- sized Commercial Banks	Joint-stock commercial banks and city commercial banks	Same as institution coverage
Joint-stock Commercial Banks	China Citic Bank, China Everbright Bank, Huaxia Bank, China Guangfa Bank, Ping An Bank, China Merchants Bank, Shanghai Pudong Development Bank, Industrial Bank, China Minsheng Banking Corporation, Evergrowing Bank, China Zheshang Bank and Bohai bank	Same as institution coverage

continued

Terms	Coverage of institutions	Statistical coverage of institutions
Banking Asset Management Companies	China Huarong Asset Management Co., Ltd., China Great Wall Asset Management Corporation, China Orient Asset Management Corporation, and China　Cinda Asset Management Co., Ltd.	Same as institution coverage
Non-bank Financial Institutions	Trust companies, finance companies of corporate groups, financial leasing companies, money brokerage firms, auto financing companies and consumer finance companies	Same as institution coverage
Small- and Medium-Sized Rural Financial Institutions	Rural cooperative financial institutions and new-type rural financial institutions	na
Rural Cooperative Financial Institutions	Rural credit cooperatives, rural cooperative banks, rural commercial banks	Same as institution coverage
New-type Rural Financial Institutions	Village or township banks, lending companies, rural mutual cooperatives	Same as institution coverage

Photograph by the CBRC staff

Part Eleven

CBRC
Annual Report
2014

Statistics

- Total assets of banking institutions (2003–2014)
- Total liabilities of banking institutions (2003–2014)
- Total owner's equity of banking institutions (2003–2014)
- Total deposits and loans of banking institutions (2003–2014)
- Profit after tax of banking institutions (2007–2014)
- Returns of banking institutions (2007–2014)
- NPLs of banking institutions (2010–2014)
- Liquidity ratio of banking institutions (2007–2014)

......

Appendix 1 Total assets of banking institutions (2003-2014)

Unit: RMB 100 million

Institutions/Year	2003	2004	2005	2006	2007	2008	2009	2010	2011	2012	2013	2014
Banking institutions	276,584	315,990	374,697	439,500	531,160	631,515	795,146	953,053	1,132,873	1,336,224	1,513,547	1,723,355
Policy banks & the CDB	21,247	24,123	29,283	34,732	42,781	56,454	69,456	76,521	93,133	112,174	125,278	156,140
Large commercial banks	160,512	179,817	210,050	242,364	285,000	325,751	407,998	468,943	536,336	600,401	656,005	710,141
Joint-stock commercial banks	29,599	36,476	44,655	54,446	72,742	88,337	118,181	149,037	183,794	235,271	269,361	313,801
City commercial banks	14,622	17,056	20,367	25,938	33,405	41,320	56,800	78,526	99,845	123,469	151,778	180,842
Rural commercial banks	385	565	3,029	5,038	6,097	9,291	18,661	27,670	42,527	62,751	85,218	115,273
Rural cooperative banks	—	—	2,750	4,654	6,460	10,033	12,791	15,002	14,025	12,835	12,322	9,570
Urban credit cooperatives	1,468	1,787	2,033	1,831	1,312	804	272	22	30	—	—	—
Rural credit cooperatives	26,509	30,767	31,427	34,503	43,434	52,113	54,945	63,911	72,047	79,535	85,951	88,312
Non-bank financial institutions	9,100	8,727	10,162	10,594	9,717	11,802	15,504	20,896	26,067	32,299	39,681	50,123
Foreign banks	4,160	5,823	7,155	9,279	12,525	13,448	13,492	17,423	21,535	23,804	25,628	27,921
New-type rural financial institutions & Postal savings bank	8,984	10,850	13,787	16,122	17,687	22,163	27,045	35,101	43,536	53,511	62,110	70,981

Notes: Data for 2003 to 2006 refer to the combined assets of banking institutions within China.

Data for 2007 to 2014 refer to the consolidated assets of banking institutions within and outside China.

Appendix 2   Total liabilities of banking institutions (2003-2014)

Unit: RMB 100 million

Institutions/ Year	2003	2004	2005	2006	2007	2008	2009	2010	2011	2012	2013	2014
Banking institutions	265,945	303,253	358,070	417,106	500,763	593,614	750,706	894,731	1,060,779	1,249,515	1,411,830	1,600,222
Policy banks & the CDB	20,291	23,005	27,760	33,006	39,203	52,648	65,393	72,159	88,231	106,647	118,966	148,704
Large commercial banks	154,002	172,180	200,453	228,824	269,176	306,142	386,036	440,332	502,591	560,879	611,611	657,135
Joint-stock commercial banks	28,621	35,333	43,320	52,542	69,350	83,924	112,541	140,872	173,000	222,130	253,438	294,641
City commercial banks	14,123	16,473	19,540	24,723	31,521	38,651	53,213	73,703	93,203	115,395	141,804	168,372
Rural commercial banks	380	538	2,873	4,789	5,767	8,756	17,546	25,643	39,208	57,841	78,492	105,954
Rural cooperative banks	—	—	2,574	4,359	6,050	9,381	11,940	13,887	12,959	11,796	11,232	8,732
Urban credit cooperatives	1,464	1,766	2,001	1,781	1,247	757	255	21	24	—	—	—
Rural credit cooperatives	26,646	30,035	30,106	33,005	41,567	49,893	52,601	61,118	68,575	75,521	81,434	83,270
Non-bank financial institutions	7,683	7,745	9,126	9,424	7,961	9,492	12,649	17,063	21,310	26,194	31,952	40,384
Foreign banks	3,751	5,329	6,530	8,532	11,353	12,028	11,818	15,569	19,431	21,249	22,896	24,832
New-type rural financial institutions & Postal savings bank	8,984	10,850	13,787	16,122	17,568	21,942	26,713	34,365	42,247	51,712	59,812	67,972

Notes: Data for 2003 to 2006 refer to the combined assets of banking institutions within China.

Data for 2007 to 2014 refer to the consolidated assets of banking institutions within and outside China.

Appendix 3   Total owner's equity of banking institutions (2003-2014)

Unit: RMB 100 million

Institutions/ Year	2003	2004	2005	2006	2007	2008	2009	2010	2011	2012	2013	2014
Banking institutions	10,639	12,737	16,627	22,394	30,396	37,900	44,441	58,322	72,094	86,708	101,716	123,132
Policy banks & the CDB	957	1,118	1,523	1,726	3,578	3,806	4,063	4,363	4,902	5,527	6,312	7,436
Large commercial banks	6,509	7,637	9,597	13,540	15,824	19,608	21,962	28,611	33,745	39,522	44,394	53,006
Joint-stock commercial banks	977	1,143	1,335	1,904	3,392	4,414	5,640	8,166	10,794	13,142	15,922	19,161
City commercial banks	499	584	827	1,215	1,883	2,669	3,587	4,822	6,641	8,075	9,974	12,470
Rural commercial banks	5	27	156	249	330	534	1,115	2,026	3,320	4,910	6,726	9,318
Rural cooperative banks	—	—	177	295	410	653	851	1,115	1,066	1,039	1,090	838
Urban credit cooperatives	4	20	32	50	64	47	17	2	5	—	—	—
Rural credit cooperatives	-137	732	1,320	1,497	1,867	2,220	2,344	2,793	3,471	4,014	4,517	5,042
Non-bank financial institutions	1,417	982	1,036	1,170	1,756	2,310	2,855	3,833	4,757	6,105	7,728	9,738
Foreign banks	408	494	625	747	1,172	1,420	1,674	1,854	2,104	2,555	2,732	3,089
New-type rural financial institutions & Postal savings bank	0	0	0	0	120	221	332	736	1,289	1,799	2,297	3,009

Notes: Data for 2003 to 2006 refer to the combined assets of banking institutions within China.

Data for 2007 to 2014 refer to the consolidated assets of banking institutions within and outside China.

Appendix 4   Total deposits and loans of banking institutions (2003-2014)

Unit: RMB 100 million

Items/Year	2003	2004	2005	2006	2007	2008	2009	2010	2011	2012	2013	2014
Total deposits	220,364	254,089	300,209	348,065	401,051	478,444	612,006	733,382	826,701	943,102	1,070,588	1,173,735
Saving deposits	110,695	126,196	147,054	166,617	176,213	221,503	264,761	307,166	347,401	403,704	451,827	489,798
Total loans	169,771	189,411	206,838	238,519	277,747	320,129	425,597	509,226	581,893	672,875	766,327	867,868
Domestic short-term loans	87,398	90,808	91,157	101,762	118,898	128,609	151,353	171,237	217,480	268,152	311,773	336,371
Domestic medium- & long-term loans	67,252	81,007	92,941	113,173	138,581	164,195	235,579	305,128	333,747	363,894	410,346	471,818
Domestic bill financing	9,234	11,622	16,319	17,333	12,884	19,314	23,879	14,845	15,154	20,447	19,616	29,233

Note: Data are from the People's Bank of China.

Appendix 5   Profit after tax of banking institutions (2007-2014)

Unit: RMB 100 million

Institutions/Year	2007	2008	2009	2010	2011	2012	2013	2014
Banking institutions	4,467.3	5,833.6	6,684.2	8,990.9	12,518.7	15,115.5	17,444.6	19,277.4
Policy banks & the CDB	489.3	229.8	352.5	415.2	536.7	736.3	922.1	1,079.6
Large commercial banks	2,466.0	3,542.2	4,001.2	5,151.2	6,646.6	7,545.8	8,382.3	8,897.5
Joint-stock commercial banks	564.4	841.4	925.0	1,358.0	2,005.0	2,526.3	2,945.4	3,211.1
City commercial banks	248.1	407.9	496.5	769.8	1,080.9	1,367.6	1,641.4	1,859.5
Rural commercial banks	42.8	73.2	149.0	279.9	512.2	782.8	1,070.1	1,383.0
Rural cooperative banks	54.5	103.6	134.9	179.0	181.9	172.2	162.1	125.5
Urban credit cooperatives	7.7	6.2	1.9	0.1	0.2	—	—	—
Rural credit cooperatives	193.4	219.1	227.9	232.9	531.2	654.0	729.2	829.8
Non-bank financial institutions	333.8	284.5	298.7	408.0	598.8	825.5	1,059.7	1,265.2
Foreign banks	60.8	119.2	64.5	77.8	167.3	163.4	140.3	197.2
New-type rural financial institutions & Postal savings bank	6.5	6.5	32.2	119.0	257.9	340.7	390.3	427.3

Appendix 6   Returns of banking institutions (2007-2014)

Unit: percent

Items/Year	2007	2008	2009	2010	2011	2012	2013	2014
Banking institutions								
Return on asset	0.9	1.0	0.9	1.0	1.2	1.2	1.2	1.2
Return on equity	16.7	17.1	16.2	17.5	19.2	19.0	18.5	17.1
Commercial banks								
Return on asset	0.9	1.1	1.0	1.1	1.3	1.3	1.3	1.2
Return on equity	16.7	19.5	18.0	19.2	20.4	19.8	19.2	17.6

Appendix 7   NPLs of banking institutions (2010-2014)

Unit: RMB 100 million, percent

Items/Year	2010	2011	2012	2013	2014
Outstanding balance of NPLs	**12,437.0**	**10,533.4**	**10,746.3**	**11,762.7**	**14,334.7**
Substandard	5,852.5	4,784.3	5,270.6	5,649.4	7,295.2
Doubtful	4,967.8	4,400.9	4,386.7	4,899.4	5,639.3
Loss	1,616.7	1,348.1	1,089.0	1,213.9	1,400.2
NPL ratio	**2.4**	**1.8**	**1.6**	**1.5**	**1.6**
Substandard	1.1	0.8	0.8	0.7	0.8
Doubtful	1.0	0.7	0.6	0.6	0.6
Loss	0.3	0.2	0.2	0.2	0.2

Appendix 8   Liquidity ratio of banking institutions (2007-2014)

Unit: percent

Items/Year	2007	2008	2009	2010	2011	2012	2013	2014
Banking institutions	40.3	49.8	45.7	43.7	44.7	47.8	46.0	48.4
Commercial banks	37.7	46.1	42.4	42.2	43.2	45.8	44.0	46.4

Appendix 9   NPLs, asset impairment provisions and provisioning coverage ratio of commercial banks (2007-2014)

Unit: RMB 100 million, percent

Items/Year	2007	2008	2009	2010	2011	2012	2013	2014
Outstanding balance of NPLs	12,701.9	5,635.4	5,066.8	4,336.0	4,278.7	4,928.5	5,921.3	8,425.6
Substandard	2,192.3	2,640.0	2,112.0	1,619.3	1,725.2	2,176.2	2,537.8	4,031.0
Doubtful	4,626.2	2,419.1	2,320.5	2,052.2	1,883.5	2,122.4	2,574.1	3,403.0
Loss	5,883.3	576.2	634.3	664.5	670.1	630.0	809.4	991.6
NPL ratio	6.1	2.4	1.6	1.1	1.0	1.0	1.0	1.2
Substandard	1.0	1.1	0.7	0.4	0.4	0.4	0.4	0.6
Doubtful	2.2	1.0	0.7	0.5	0.4	0.4	0.4	0.5
Loss	2.8	0.2	0.2	0.2	0.2	0.1	0.1	0.1
Asset impairment provisions	6,029.6	7,801.4	8,750.5	10,308.1	12,677.1	15,307.9	17,551.1	20,686.5
Provisioning coverage ratio	41.4	116.6	153.2	217.7	278.1	295.5	282.7	232.1

Appendix 10   NPLs of commercial banks (2014)

Unit: RMB 100 million, percent

Items/Institutions	Commercial banks in total	Large commercial banks	Joint-stock commercial banks	City commercial banks	Rural commercial banks	Foreign banks
Outstanding balance of NPLs	8,425.6	4,764.9	1,618.6	855.4	1,090.5	96.2
Substandard	4,031.0	2,119.9	885.3	465.1	524.9	35.7
Doubtful	3,403.0	2,038.3	518.9	275.4	523.0	47.3
Loss	991.6	606.6	214.3	114.8	42.6	13.2
NPL ratio	1.2	1.2	1.1	1.2	1.9	0.8
Substandard	0.6	0.5	0.6	0.6	0.9	0.3
Doubtful	0.5	0.5	0.4	0.4	0.9	0.4
Loss	0.1	0.2	0.1	0.2	0.1	0.1

Appendix 11   Distribution of NPLs of commercial banks by industry (2014)

Unit: RMB 100 million, percent

Industries/Items	Outstanding balance	NPL ratio
A Agriculture Forestry, Animal Husbandry and Fishing	388.3	2.64
B Mining	181.6	1.04
C Manufacturing	3,035.6	2.42
D Production and Supply of Electricity, Gas and Water	98.6	0.34
E Construction	214.3	0.72
F Wholesale and Retail Trade	2,695.0	3.05
G Transport, Storage and Post	274.3	0.52
H Lodging and Catering Services	104.8	1.47
I Information Transmission, Computer Services and Software	36.0	1.15
J Financial Services	8.1	0.21
K Real Estate	263.3	0.50
L Leasing and Business Services	107.2	0.33
M Scientific Research, Technical Services	9.2	0.66
N Management of Water Conservancy, Environment and Public Facilities	18.4	0.08
O Services to Households, Maintenance and Other Services	50.4	1.43
P Education	17.3	0.58
Q Health and Social Work	3.4	0.11
R Culture, Sports and Entertainment	13.6	0.65
S Public Management, Social Security and Social Organization	6.4	0.25
T International Organizations	0.2	3.80
Personal Loans (excluding personal business loans)	882.3	0.62
Credit Card	387.7	1.49
Automobiles	27.0	2.07
Home Mortgage Loans	290.5	0.29
Other Personal Loans	177.0	1.19

Appendix 12 Distribution of NPLs of commercial banks by region (2014)

Unit: RMB 100 million, percent

Districts/Items	Outstanding balance	NPL ratio
Headquarters	418.3	1.49
Eastern region	5,418.2	1.35
Beijing	293.0	0.72
Tianjin	190.6	1.11
Hebei	146.2	0.74
Liaoning	362.6	1.46
Shanghai	370.7	1.02
Jiangsu	848.0	1.31
Zhejiang	1,219.9	2.04
Fujian	454.1	1.94
Shandong	716.8	1.72
Guangdong	802.2	1.15
Hainan	14.2	0.55
Central region	1,359.1	1.28
Shanxi	196.4	1.70
Jilin	93.3	1.14
Heilongjiang	110.0	1.55
Anhui	219.1	1.30
Jiangxi	158.3	1.44
Henan	178.5	0.97
Hubei	236.7	1.28
Hunan	166.8	1.16
Western region	1,215.2	1.05
Chongqing	75.9	0.46
Sichuan	319.8	1.26
Guizhou	82.0	0.97
Yunnan	107.8	0.94
Tibet	3.5	0.23
Shaanxi	143.1	1.08
Gansu	25.3	0.47
Qinghai	25.3	1.00
Ningxia	37.5	1.20
Xinjiang	60.0	0.84
Guangxi	113.8	1.13
Inner Mongolia	221.2	2.16
Total (domestic)	8,410.7	1.29
Total (overseas branches)	14.8	0.06

Appendix 13 CAR of commercial banks (2010-2014)

Unit: RMB 100 million, percent

Items/Year	2010	2011	2012
Core capital	42,985.1	53,366.6	64,340.1
Supplementary capital	10,294.5	14,417.6	17,585.1
Capital deductions	3,196.4	3,735.4	4,057.1
On-balance sheet risk-weighted assets	355,371.1	431,420.7	506,604.1
Off-balance sheet risk-weighted assets	53,233.7	68,819.0	76,108.0
Market risk capital	273.3	296.3	388.4
CAR	12.2	12.7	13.3
Core CAR	10.1	10.2	10.6

Appendix 14 CAR of commercial banks (2013-2014)

Unit: RMB 100 million, percent

Items/Year	2013	2014
Net core tier one capital	75,793.2	90,738.6
Net tier one capital	75,793.2	92,480.8
Net capital	92,856.1	113,269.3
Reputation risk-weighted asset	696,582.6	763,911.1
Market risk-weighted asset	6,066.5	6,845.4
Operation risk-weighted asset	59,124.0	68,193.5
Core tier one CAR	9.9	10.6
Tier one CAR	9.9	10.8
CAR	12.2	13.2

Note: *The Administrative Measures for the Capital of Commercial Banks (for Trial Implementation*) was implemented on January 1, 2013, and the original *the Administrative Measures for the Capital Adequacy Ratio of Commercial Banks* was abolished at the same time. As a result, since the first quarter of 2013, the related statistics of CAR released in the appendix was calculated according to the New Measures.

Appendix 15   CBRC on-site examinations (2003-2014)

Unit: RMB 100 million, Number of banks, person, percent

Items/Year	2003	2004	2005	2006	2007	2008	2009	2010	2011	2012	2013	2014
Funds involved in illegal transactions	1,768	5,840	7,671	10,147	8,555	12,883	11,514	15,370	12,634	11,565	23,165	51,001
Number of banking institutions which received penalties on rule-breaking activities	1,512	2,202	1,205	1,104	1,360	873	4212	2,312	1,977	1,553	1,341	2,157
Number of senior managerial personnel with qualifications revoked	257	244	325	243	177	78	86	49	66	55	38	22
Average institutional coverage ratio of onsite examinations	28	36	34	35	42	24	30	27	19	20	16	15

Appendix 16   Number of legal entities and staff of banking institutions (As of end-2014)

Unit: Person, number of banks

Institutions / Items	Number of staff	Number of banks
Large commercial banks	1,764,617	5
Policy banks and the CDB	62,520	3
Joint-stock commercial banks	410,816	12
City commercial banks	346,816	133
Rural credit cooperatives	423,992	1,596
Rural commercial banks	373,635	665
Rural cooperative banks	32,614	89
Finance companies of corporate groups	9,095	196
Trust companies	16,683	68
Financial leasing companies	2,851	30
Auto financing companies	6,072	18
Money brokerage firms	605	5
Consumer finance companies	11,871	6
Banking asset management companies	8,399	4
Foreign financial institutions	47,412	41
Other institutions	245,437	1,218
Banking institutions in total	3,763,435	4,089

Note: Other institutions include new type rural financial institutions, Postal Savings Bank of China and Sino-German Bausparkasse.

Chief Editor of this Annual Report: YANG Jiacai

Executive Editors:YANG Dongning, YIN Xiaobei, ZHANG Xianqiu, HU Meijun, WANG Fei, GAN Yu, SONG Lijian, JIA Jinglei, LI Hanyang, ZHANG Jing, LI li, CHENG Gengli, ZHANG Jingjing, DONG Su, LI Xinghao, LUO Xuyao, HAO Li, HUANG Xinxin, GAN Zhi.

Editors of the English version of this Annual Report:ZHANG Lixing, LU Wei, WU Jie, LI Wei, ZHANG Lu, PAN Yun, ZHU Ling, WU Hao, ZHANG Lingyu, FU Chaohuan.

This Annual Report also benefits from the work of ZHEN Jinyu, LIU Moran, WEI Aijun, JIANG Fengsen, LIU Xingfei, WANG Cui, YAO Ge, QI Yali, HE Xiaolin, WANG Yun, CHEN Ken, LIN Wanbao, LIANG Jianlin, GAO Song, HU Han, LI Wei, LI Shiyang, LIU Biyun, HUANG Haosheng.

The photographs inserted in this Annual Report are contributed by the CBRC staff:CHEN Wenxiong, HE Wenwen, SHAN Jijin, SHI Suoyun, YANG Xiaochun, YI Zhou, WANG Chao, WANG Guanyi, WANG Yang, WANG Zhenyuan, ZHANG Baocheng, ZHOU Minyuan.Special thanks to all of them.